Jean-Baptiste Morin

Astrologia Gallica
Book Seventeen

The Astrological Houses

Translated from the Latin
By
James Herschel Holden, M.A.

Fellow of the American
Federation of Astrologers

First Printing 2008

ISBN-10: 0-86690-583-9
ISBN-13: 978-0-86690-583-1

Published by:
American Federation of Astrologers, Inc.
6535 S. Rural Road
Tempe, AZ 85283

www.astrologers.com

Printed in the United States of America

This book is for all Students
of the Morin Method.

Contents

Translator's Preface

In *Astrologia Gallica*, Book 17, Section I, Morin takes up the matter of the twelve houses of the astrological chart. He first states the nature of the division of the *Caelum* into houses and then deals with the criticisms levied by opponents of astrology, who declared that the division of the *Caelum* into 12 houses and the assignment of individual characteristics to them was purely arbitrary and without any rational foundation. Not so, says Morin, and he gives his reasons for contradicting their objections.

Some parts of this Section closely resemble Morin's statements in his early book, *The Cabala of the Twelve Houses*.[1] But both there and here the word *Cabala* is misleading. At first glance it would seem to imply that Morin had found something in the Jewish Kabbalah that pertained to the astrological houses, but that is not so. There is no mention of the Kabbalah. Instead, he seems to have used the word *Cabala* as a more exotic synonym of the word *Mystery*.

And even *mystery* is an overstatement. The mystery seems to consist of the fact that in his opinion the signification of the houses can be deduced by counting them from the ASC in both the clockwise and counter-clockwise directions. The clockwise direction (ASC, 12, 11, 10, etc.) is the direction of the diurnal motion of the Planets, while the counter-clockwise direction (the familiar ASC, 2, 3, IMC, etc.) is the direction in which the Planets move through the zodiac.

What Morin actually does is to give what seemed to him to be valid reasons why the celestial houses can be arranged in

---

[1] *Astrologicarum domorum cabala detecta a Joanne Baptista Morino...* [The Cabala of the Astrological Houses Discovered by Jean Baptiste Morin ...] (Paris: J. Moreau, 1623. 8vo 38 pp.). There is a 17th century translation by the English astrologer Sir George Wharton, *The Cabal of the Twelve Houses* (1659), which can now be read online at www.skyscript.co.uk/cabal.

triplicities similar to the arrangement of the signs of the zodiac into *trigons* (he seems to prefer that word for them). By assigning general characteristics to these celestial triplicities, Morin sets forth what he believes to be reasons for the characteristics of the individual houses. His assignments are mainly like the traditional ones inherited from the earliest Western astrologers,[1] with the exception of the characteristics of the 6th and 12th houses.

In the case of the 6th house, he assigns servants and animals to it, while he assigns illnesses and other bodily problems to the 12th house. But he also says that the 4th house rules both parents, not just the father. And he stresses the point that each house shares the characteristics of its opposite house to a lesser degree—this, he says, is why previous astrologers mistakenly assigned illness to the 6th house. It does relate frequently to illness, but since it is opposite the real house of illness, the 12th, it does so in a secondary way.

In Section I, Chapter 8, Morin embarks on a lengthy inquiry into whether the bad houses of the horoscope, the 6th, the 8th and the 12th, would have had their present signification before Adam's sin. Since Adam was the first man, the question could only have applied to him and to his wife Eve. And since it is purely theoretical, it hardly seems to us today to have been worth considering. But this question seemed to be important to Morin, and so he had a lot to say about it. Perhaps his main contention is that the houses, the domiciles, and the planets had the same significations before Adam's fall from grace as afterwards. For us in the twenty-first century, this is scarcely a matter of any importance, but the patient reader may marvel at the intricacies of thought that are presented in this lengthy chapter.

---

[1]The Alexandrian astrologers, who invented horoscopic astrology in the 2nd century B.C., assigned characteristics to each of the 12 houses according to some logical scheme that has unfortunately not come down to us, since the earliest astrological treatises are lost, and their contents are only partially and imperfectly known from citations by later Classical astrologers. The lack of the original rationale enabled later critics of astrology to assert that the assignments were arbitrary and therefore valueless. To counter this, Morin endeavors to establish a rational basis for the assignments.

Section II contains a technical discussion of several systems of House division. Morin begins by attacking the Equal House System of House Division, first offering theoretical arguments against it, and then presenting several horoscopes drawn in the so-called Rational System of Regiomontanus[1] and pointing out that the house positions of the planets in that system are more in accordance with the facts of the Natives' lives than their positions in the Equal House System.

Like Regiomontanus, he asserts that Ptolemy had the Regiomontanus System in mind in *Tetrabiblos*, Book 3, Chapter 10. But this is not true, since what Ptolemy mentioned was only a minor variation of the Equal House System. Morin does not mention the Placidus System of house division in this book, since it was probably already written before Placidus's books were published. However, in AG Book 23, Chapter 16, he does mention it and calls it "false and erroneous," since it rejected the circles of position that are employed in the Regiomontanus system.

Morin next offers what seemed to him to be valid arguments in favor of viewing the equator as the primary circle to be divided. And he says that those systems that only divide the ecliptic in various ways cannot therefore be true. He then mentions the Campanus System and shows his own horoscope with Campanus cusps, but he also votes against that system.

Finally, he explains his own system, which is now called the Morinus System, and shows his chart drawn in that system. He notes that the signs on the cusps of two of the houses have changed, which changes the planetary rulers of those houses, and he then discusses the changes in interpretation that result from that, but he asserts that the revised interpretations are also valid. His conclusion is that the Morinus System is a valid one.

However, we may note that since the changes in house position

---

[1] It was dubbed "Rational" because it was supposed to have the most reasonable theoretical basis.

in his own chart were minor, this does not seem to be a fair test of the system. If he had redrawn the charts of Wallenstein or Gustavus Adolphus, there would have been drastic changes. And it should also be noted that the Morinus System does not produce the true ASC degree, which all astrologers from the Alexandrian founders down to the present time have considered to be a point of prime significance in the horoscope. In fact, the Morinus System does not even produce the true astronomical MC degree. Consequently, it is clearly wrong.

If the student has already chosen a house system (such as Placidus) and is satisfied with it, he can probably skip over the technical parts of Section II, since they mainly deal with the technical details of house division used in the various systems, and since it is primarily a defense of the Regiomontanus System. However, the charts that are given as examples should be studied.

Section III continues the discussion of the houses. Chapter 2 states that the calculations should be made for a point on the surface of the Earth rather than for its center, and Morin actually mentions that this can make a noticeable change in the apparent longitude of the Moon. He thus seems to advocate the application of the parallax correction to the Moon's position. However, he does not seem to have ever done this in practice. Chapter 5 is followed by two Problems that explain how Morin calculated cuspal distances and converse primary directions to planets in the 12th house and the 9th house for the rectification of the birth time. These are quite technical, and have mostly a historical interest.

As I have done in my translations of other books of the *Astrologia Gallica*, I have tried to turn Morin's scholarly Latin into readable English as literally as possible. But he had a large vocabulary, and rather than attempting to match him by studding the English sentences with uncommon words, I have used more common renderings of seldom encountered Latin words. I have also tried to keep paraphrase to a minimum.

Also, as previously, I have retained the Latin word *Caelum* 'sky' as a technical term; it refers to the zodiac and the placement of the Sun, Moon, planets, and fixed stars in it at a particular moment. I have also retained *Primum Caelum* 'first sky', which refers to the supposed outer sphere of the universe more commonly called *Primum Mobile*, which contains the signs of the zodiac And the reader will find that in this book (from p. 31 on) Morin frequently uses the word "space" as a synonym for "house."

As a writer, Morin resembles a college professor teaching a course in astrology. He talks extensively about each topic that he introduces, explaining the background and the justifications of the rules that he introduces. From time to time he even raises objections to the rules and refutes them. And he cites the rules that some of his predecessors have stated and discusses them. Thus, the reader not only learns what Morin believed to be true, but he is also introduced to some alternative theories that were current in the 17th century. Some of this may seem excessive, but Morin took great pains to discuss all aspects of his topics.

If this is the first book of the *Astrologia Gallica* that the reader has taken up, he will be immediately struck by the length of some of the sentences. Morin sometimes extends a sentence into half of a page. His idea of the proper length of a paragraph also differs considerably from ours, so I have broken some of the solid text into paragraphs. And I have occasionally broken up some of his long sentences into two or more shorter ones, but more often I have kept them together with commas, semi-colons, and dashes. I have occasionally used italics to emphasize a word where Morin did not, and I have added some words in brackets where I thought they were needed.

Also, the reader may find that after having read one of Morin's extra long sentences, he is uncertain whether he has understood it. In such a case, my advice is to read it again and think about how the several clauses fit together. Morin is not an especially easy author. He should not be skimmed. To derive the maximum benefit from what he has to say, it may be necessary to re-read some parts of it and think about them. Unlike most astrological writers, Morin does not simply state a rule, but as mentioned above he also discusses the reasons for the rule and objections that have been raised against it.

One feature of Morin's discussion that is seldom encountered in modern astrological texts is his quotations from the Bible and his not infrequent digressions into religious or philosophical justifications of the rules and explanations that he sets forth. Morin was a devout Catholic, and he was at pains to try to show that nothing in his book was contrary to Catholic dogma. This was partly due to the sincerity of his personal religious beliefs and partly due to a desire to avoid giving religious opponents of astrology obvious targets to attack. But he also tried to find Biblical justification for some of his explanations or procedures.

The reader will also find frequent references to Claudius Ptolemy's *Tetrabiblos* (or *Quadripartite*, as the Latin translation was called). Morin seems to have generally cited the Latin version printed by Jerome Cardan in his voluminous *Commentary on the Quadripartite*. Since the numbering of the chapters in that text does not agree exactly with those in F.E. Robbins's edition and translation of the *Tetrabiblos* in the Loeb Classical Library, I have generally changed the chapter numbers cited by Morin to agree with the chapter numbers in the LCL version.

And I have sometimes expanded Morin's citations of passages in Cardan's book to agree with the numbering in the Lyons omnibus edition of Cardan's works published in 1663. (Morin of course used an earlier edition, which I have not seen.) I do not have access to all of the books by the other authors that Morin mentions from time to time, so I am unable to augment his references to those. I have, however, supplied references to their place and date of publication.

It will soon become obvious to the reader that Morin usually cites Ptolemy or Cardan only in order to disagree with their statements. In the 17th century they were considered to be the two leading authorities on astrology. And, since Morin had devised a system of astrology that differed in important respects from the tradition set forth by his two eminent predecessors, he felt obliged to point out the differences and explain why he thought that his system was preferable.

He particularly cites numerous passages from Cardan and delivers what he believes to be logical arguments against them. And he also cites passages from Jofrancus Offusius (16th century) in order to show that from his point of view they too were erroneous. Offusius, like Morin, had discarded a good bit of traditional astrology and substituted a system of his own devising. But not surprisingly, Morin thought that his own system was better than Offusius's, and he goes into detail to explain why. I think the reader will agree with him.

However, we must remember that Ptolemy, Cardan, and Offusius all lived before the invention of the telescope. Consequently, some of their statements relating to the structure of the solar system, while generally believed to be correct as late as the end of the 16th century, were found to be incorrect in the early 17th century. And while Morin accepted Kepler's elliptical orbits for the planets, he refused to give up the idea that the Earth was the center of the universe, since he was a devout Catholic, and the Church had not yet abandoned that erroneous belief.

Still, it is important to note that since horoscopes are calculated with geocentric positions regardless of how those positions are calculated, Morin's method of astrological interpretation is largely unaffected by the change in astronomical theory and remains valid.

Finally, I want to thank my friend Kris Brandt Riske for converting my word-processor files into publishing files and seeing the present book through the publishing process.

James H. Holden
May 2006

Astrologia Gallica

Book Seventeen

The Astrological Houses

Preface

After having set forth the forces of the signs and the planets, as the primary fundamentals of all astrology, it now follows that we should discuss the second fundamental of astrology—namely, the astrological houses, into which the Caelum *is customarily divided for judgments. For the entire knowledge of Judicial Astrology depends upon these houses, and judgments are produced by means of their natures, as will be plain in what follows. Besides, the old astrologers and the modern ones are separated into various factions with regard to these houses; and it seems very difficult to elicit the truth (which is unique) from their diverse opinions. Nevertheless, with God's help, we shall not only find that truth, but in fact we shall establish it firmly, so that it cannot be overturned by any contrivances of adversaries after this.*

Section I.

The Cabala of the Astrological Houses and its Natural Foundation that We have Revealed.

Chapter 1. *The Whole Natural Effect from the Whole* Caelum *and its Parts Depends upon the Position Within it and the Direction of its Parts.*

That the *Primum Caelum* is the prime cause or the prime physical principle of the natural effects was sufficiently shown by us in Book 14,[1] Section I, Chapter 10; moreover, the first principle in

---

[1]*Astrologia Gallica Books Thirteen, Fourteen, Fifteen, and Nineteen* trans. by James Herschel Holden (Tempe, Az.: A.F.A., Inc., 2006).

any nativity ought to be the most perfect; it will therefore be the *Primum Caelum* in respect to the effective causes and the most universal and powerful active virtue (which is the greatest perfection of an efficient cause), so that there is no inferior corporeal cause that it does not motivate, or that its force of acting does not influence; and nothing new is generated in the whole World that this virtue does not affect.

Furthermore, since this is the way it is, there certainly should be no doubt for anyone that all that which is generated and born anew must be referred to that prime cause of it. Moreover, it can be referred either to some [particular] part of the *Caelum* or to the whole *Caelum*, but it should be referred to the whole. For the *Primum Caelum* is not the prime and most universal cause according to each of its parts, but according to the whole; therefore, any sublunar effect—that is, in its own birth, [period of] vigor, decline, and death—since it can be considered according to its entire self, should be referred to the whole *Caelum*; and yet, not in a confused manner, but in a distinct and orderly one, so that the very regular motion of that *Caelum* might exhort the individual parts of the *Caelum* to that same effect, successively presenting, effecting, and in various ways applying. For, as the whole effect and those things that happen during [a certain time] of the *Caelum* correspond to the whole *Caelum*; and yet the birth of a thing is not the death of that same thing, so that which was in the *Caelum* was per se as the cause of that birth, that same thing will not be the cause per se of its death; for [if that were] so, nothing would last—that is, the effect would not even be produced; but as birth, vigor, decline, and the death of things are different and they succeed each other, the causes of these in the *Caelum* must differ among themselves and must [also] succeed each other; but the difference and the succession are not in the *Caelum* except by reason of its parts. Therefore, there are some parts of the *Caelum* that are the causes of birth, or which preside over birth, and others succeeding these [that cause] vigor; others that are the causes of decline; and finally others that [are the causes] of the death of things.

4

Moreover, the necessity of this division can be shown in another way thus. The whole *Caelum* pours forth many and diverse influences at the same instant—at the same birth; but the same thing, as far as the same thing, cannot at the same time effect different things in the same thing. Therefore, the *Caelum*, as a whole or as an identity will not effect those different things, but as it is divided into parts, one part does this, and another part does that.

Chapter 2. *The General Division of the Natural Effects with Respect to the Whole* Caelum.

Since, therefore, being led and taught by Nature herself, shall we say that the part of the *Caelum* that is rising is the prime cause of any natural thing?—that part indeed that arises above the horizon at the birth of the thing, and arising makes that thing to rise. For it is certain that among the places of the *Caelum*, the rising is very much more powerful than the rest of the places, as all astrologers make an explanation of the rising, culmination, and setting; and experience of the changes in the air are convincing about those things. But a cause is said to be more powerful only by reason of its more elaborate and more difficult effect; therefore, the more elaborate and more difficult effect on things must be attributed to the ascending part of the *Caelum*, which no one will deny to be the birth or the bringing forth of things.

Moreover, that part of the *Caelum* that is successively more elevated above the horizon, holds the MC of the *Caelum* in the arising of the thing, claims its vigor and the ruling virtue of acting for itself; that [part] which is *falling* at the same time governs the decline of the thing from its vigor; and finally that [part] that obtains the IMC will be judged to be the cause of the corruption and death of the thing.

And this is the simplest of all and the prime division of the *Caelum*, by which all physical things are generated, increased, and altered from their own nature, and finally corrupted, and to which truly and reasonably the *Caelum* itself is adapted, which division alone the old astrologers frequently used in [both] universal and particular constitutions of the *Caelum*, as is plain from Haly's[1] [account] of the figure of the comet [that appeared] in his own time; because either from the deficiency of the astronomical tables in those times, a more minute division of the *Caelum* would be more difficult,[2] or because it would generally contain whatever another special [division] would contain.

Chapter 3. *The Special Division of the Whole* Caelum *into Twelve Astrological Houses with Respect to the Man being Born.*

Truly, since some astrologer of prime wisdom, whoever he was, yet more ancient than the others that followed him, understood that the *Caelum* was made and is in motion rather for man than for rest of the animate creatures or for the sake of the inanimate ones, and that many things suit man himself on account of his more divine nature, which things agree very little with the more ignoble natures; therefore, thanks to that man, it was reasonably judged that the whole circuit of the *Caelum* must be divided into twelve parts that he called houses, drawn through great circles from some point on the *Caelum* and cutting another great circle of the *Caelum* into that many equal parts, as will be explained in its own place. And he handed down that the first house was placed in the east and that it ruled the life of man, and that conjectural knowledge is had from it, and judgment is made about life. The second house, which follows next according to the motion of the planets,[3] rules riches; the third rules brothers; the fourth, parents; and so on with the rest, as

---

[1]The reference is to the two Halys, ʿAlî ibn abi al-Rijâl (d.c. 1040) and ʿAlî ibn Riḍwân (d. 1068), both of whom recorded a comet that was first seen on 30 April 1006. See Lynn Thorndike, *Latin Treatises on Comets Between 1238 and 1368 A.D.* (Chicago: The University of Chicago Press, 1950), pp. 14-15. The geographic latitude for which their chart of the comet is calculated would appear to be about 26 N, which is 5° S of Cairo; and perhaps this is what made Morin think that their tables were inaccurate. But more likely either the MC degree or the ASC degree was simply misstated in the text.

[2]Morin means that the calculations for the Campanus or Regiomontanus systems would have been more difficult to make than the fairly simple calculations required for Alchabitius cusps.

[4]That is, in the order of the signs of the zodiac—the counter-clockwise direction.

6

they are arranged and named in the figure of the houses below.

And the name of this division of the *Caelum* and the houses has not endured uncorrupted from him down to us[1]; although Ptolemy and the others who followed him seem to disagree with that old tradition and to pervert that division in many places, such as when they mainly judge about children, not from the fifth house, but from the one opposed to it, the eleventh; and about servants and animals, not from the sixth, but from its opposite, the twelfth; which apparent error we have corrected below, not withstanding the division of the *Caelum* established in various ways by different astrologers.

The Order and Names of the Astrological Houses.

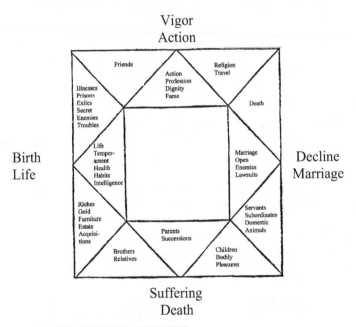

7

Moreover, it happens the same in astrology as in all the other sciences—indeed, Theology itself not excepted—that certainly, as various heresies and various marvels of sects are born in it, and superstitions are introduced, with many fictions depending on no real foundation, and yet from which it is believed that real efficiencies are produced; but from which at various times universal astrology is made known by those ignorant of that same error, falsehood, vanity, and superstition, or openly by those who hate it. And for that reason there came forth that most powerful storm that Alexander de Angelis [1562-1620], the Prefect of Studies in the Roman College of the Society of Jesus, treading on the footsteps of Pico Mirandola [1463-1494][1] and raging against astrology in five books,[2] [namely that], there cannot be any forecast of any sort of future physical events from the stars, but also that there are no [individual] parts of the *Caelum* [active] in the production of physical things, and he will not blush at asserting and maintaining that nothing is done on inferior things, that is not done by sublunar causes that are indeed close and elemental; and he has proposed that those same elements preserve themselves without any aid from the *Caelum*; and consequently the creation by the Divine Wisdom of so many distinct celestial bodies with diverse natures and motions among themselves for us living in the elementary region, and in the rest of the sublunar regions, makes a frustrating and absolute superfluity.

But this outstanding doctrine (which we have refuted elsewhere openly and by means of the prime principles of these things); from which start he held that they were not content to rave against the errors and vanities introduced into the true astrology, but they also tried to destroy the physical fundamentals of this science deliberately and with all the powers of their talent; Pico, de Angelis, Plotinus,[3] and the

[1]Count Giovanni II Pico della Mirandola, *Disputationes adversus astrologiam*. [Disputations Against Astrology], Bologna: Benedictus Hectoris, 1496.

[2]The Jesuit, Father Alexander de Angelis (Angeli, Alessandro degli), *In Astrologos coniectores. Libri Quinque.* [Conjectures Against the Astrologers. Five Books.], Lyons: H. Cardon, 1615. 4to.; Rome: B. Zanetti, 1615. 2nd ed.

[3]Famous neo-Platonic philosopher, whose Greek work, *The Enneads*, was translated into Latin in the late 15th century.

rest of that sort of philosophers, whose arguments against the true astrology propose nothing more absurd and nothing more easily overthrown, as we have already made plain elsewhere.

But among the other fundamentals of astrology, since the division into 12 houses is the first and most important, that is the one on which the whole art of predicting depends; moreover, the causes, reasons, and the first principles of this division, if they were more profoundly unknown, and if they could be contrived with very much more reasonable difficulty than the fundamentals of any other sort, in these houses surely they are only made more equal, they would transform whole mechanisms of talent, truly settled, with these overthrown, no implements of prediction [would be] surviving for astrologers. For those, moreover, it was apparently not at all difficult, since no astrologer was hitherto at home, who was able to defend those houses by true or even by probable reasons, and in this part [of astrology] Ptolemy himself was without support.

For Lucio Bellantio [d. 1499], who undertook to defend astrology against Pico Mirandola, in his 10th Book against Pico, at Book 10, Chapter 5, of that same Pico, after various [remarks], and then some nuggets from the old writings, therefore replies here to Pico, not drawing upon brevity and charm for reasons, is finally compelled to oppose a unique experience against him and to explain himself by accusations with these words that are manifest witnesses to his ignorant reasoning:

> Therefore, to seek on account of from what cause this or that house is of this [particular] virtue, is to ask why the Sun is bright, and why fire is hot, water is cold, which nevertheless depend upon intrinsic principles more unknown to us, or at least very little known.

which a little earlier he said were profound secrets of Nature.

Indeed, Kepler too, when he robbed the *Primum Caelum* of its diurnal motion, and dedicated it to the Earth,[1] did not want any force to remain in the celestial houses.

But all the rest [of the writers] who have tried to establish reasons for these houses, and especially Cardan [1501-1576], in Book 3, Chapter 1, of his Judgments of Nativities, produced nothing universal, nothing properly arranged, and nothing true, but only mere fictions; of which, if something only squared with establishing one house very closely, that same thing truly destroyed the rest of the houses. And therefore Alexander de Angelis, in Book 4, Chapter 19, after he had cited all the reasons of Julius Firmicus[2] about these houses, rightly rejected them with just these words: "He would be ridiculous who might think that these ridiculous reasons require our refutation."

Chapter 4. *The Fundamentals of that Division.*

The division of the *Caelum* into twelve small domiciles as they are discerned in the figure, must not by any means be held to be a fictitious thing stated without reason and lacking any natural foundation, but to be a most fortunate concept of the wisest intellect and the one shrewdest in the nature of things (if nevertheless any human intellect has brought it forward with its own powers, and it was not from the universal knowledge that God infused into Adam at the beginning of the World), as those things that depend upon a real foundation, the universal state of man in the *Caelum*, just as it shows it marvelously sketched out in its own first physical cause.

Moreover, this division came from its own first author to his posterity through the Cabala, who indeed by no means changed it, but nevertheless did not understand its mysteries (the spirit of the Cabala), since by no one was anything about them bequeathed to

---

[1] This refers to the fact that Kepler stated (correctly) that the Earth's daily rotation caused the *Primum Caelum* to appear to revolve about the Earth, while Morin still clung to the religious dogma that the Earth was fixed in the heavens, and the *Primum Caelum* actually rotated about it, so he thought that Kepler was wrong!

[2] The reference is to Julius Firmicus Maternus, *Matheseos libri VIII* (Leipzig; B. G. Teubner, 1968), Book 2, in which the significations of the houses are stated.

us. And in fact the full [knowledge] of the mysteries must surely be admired, whose principles were discovered by me not without unbelievable pleasure to my intellect in the year 1622, when I was returning to Paris from the siege of Montpellier,[1] to expound them, and here it is pleasing to bequeath them to posterity, although already then at the time this Cabala of the Astrological Houses was brought to the light of day by me alone,[2] as of course by the natural light in those houses, hitherto shadowy, by me first illuminated, their fancied confusion utterly vanishes, and a very beautiful and marvelous order and a scheme of order are perceived clearly by all of the imposters.

Moreover, thanks to the greater elucidation, this must be said first: namely, that the superior, prime, and simple division of the *Caelum* into four cardinal parts is not a fiction, but a natural thing, based upon a natural foundation, as was shown before. But each of these parts has two other parts in the *Caelum* of the same nature as it—namely, those with which in the divided circle it makes an equilateral triangle, or which is seen by a partile trine.

If in fact the Eternal Trinity is from infinite *love*; and it is the source and substance of the infinite and the most perfect *love*; in which the one loving, who is first, and the one loved, who is second, and the love proceeding from both of these, which is third, are *one*, not in kind or in species, but in *number*; and therefore it is the simplest and most perfect in love; and the infinite perfection of which, since it pours itself out upon all created things, more perfectly however is its analogy poured out upon itself—the sort of things that before all others are those that conform to the union of the trine; whence, therefore it is said that every trine is perfected not by some particular or special perfection, but by that first and

---

[1]The Protestant Huguenots, who held the town of Montpellier, were besieged by the army of the Catholic King Louis XIII [1601-1643], which captured the town in 1622.

[2]Here Morin refers to his book, *Astrologicarum domorum cabala detecta a Joanne Baptista Morino...* [The Cabala of the Astrological Houses Discovered by Jean Baptiste Morin ...] (Paris: J. Moreau, 1623. 8vo 38 pp.). See the note to the Preface.

most universal perfection of the *first trine*, which consists of *love*, and in which all the trines participate in various ways with the capacity of their own nature.

Therefore, since the planets repeatedly see themselves by various aspects in the celestial circles according to their various motions, that is by sextile, square, trine, and opposition, the first and wise astrologers, both by reasons obscurely taken at least a priori, namely by the infinite and most universal perfection of the first trine, and a posteriori, namely by the most evident effects that they produce; in general, the trine is the most perfect, and in it there is the perfection of the first trine, that is love thrives thus, so that the aspect was said by them to be one of perfect friendship.

Which, since nothing can be done without the similarity of natures, or at least without a generic identity, from that they rightly deduced the parts of the divided circle established in partile trine to be at least generically of the same nature, and a triplicity to be composed of that same nature; therefore, for that cause, since any one of the four superior cardinal points of the *Caelum* claims for itself a particular triplicity of its own nature (because each one of these sees the other two by a trine aspect within the divided circle), by these four triplicities the *Caelum* was divided into twelve parts which they call domiciles; and not into more nor less parts, brought from the created quaternary into the divine ternary division, it was divisible; and therefore this division was held to be absolutely and entirely perfect.

Chapter 5. *The Explanation of that Division, and its Marvelous and Greatly Reasonable Application to all those things that Occur During the Life of that Man.*

Having explained the previous things, I say now that the life of man consists of four ages, childhood, youth, virility, and old age. And in man four different ones are discerned, to which all the rest of [the accidents] of that man are reduced, just as they are to his own principal categories—namely, *life*, *action*, *marriage*, and *suf-*

fering. Moreover, these coincide with *birth, vigor, decline,* and *death*, which four agree universally with all the effects of nature that we have mentioned previously.

For man is said to arise in this manner: since first he enjoys a mundane life per se; he flourishes in the act when he does act as a man, or he converts his own vigor of acting reasonably into an act; he declines when he has a foreboding of his own inability to perpetuate himself, and yet from an innate desire for perpetuity, he begins to join himself to another person, so that he can attain it in some manner; and finally he dies when he encounters the last suffering of his life.

Therefore, man's life, action, marriage, and suffering pertain to the same celestial principle as the birth, vigor, decline and death of things in general—namely, life at the ASC, action at the MC, marriage at the DSC, and [the last] suffering at the IMC. But from [a consideration of] this, there arise **four triplicities** of the same generic nature, and twelve houses, as [mentioned] above.

And indeed the **First Triplicity** is the one of the ASC angle, which they call the first house; and it pertains to childhood; and it is called the triplicity of *being* and *life*; and the other houses of this triplicity are the ninth and the fifth, which in the circle with which there is a reasonable division of the houses, they aspect the first house with a partile trine. Moreover, man lives in a threefold manner—in himself, in God, and in his children—indeed, *life* is first only given to man on account of other things—namely, he worships God, and he generates likenesses of himself, which is the complete intention of God for the production of man.

But now, the life of man [begins] in himself—because of the other things this is the **first** in the order of nature, and without which the others cannot exist—therefore, it rightly lays claim for itself to be the principal house of this triplicity, that is the rising angle, along with the other things pertaining to life itself, that is the constitution of the body, health, habits, and intelligence, of which the causes and signs may be determined from this house.

The life in God, the **second** in order, exists in the House of Religion, that is the ninth, the first house of this triplicity that follows [the ASC] according to the motion of the equator.[1]

Finally, the life in children is assigned to the fifth house, which is the House of Children. This whole triplicity, therefore, is one of *life*, but it seems to be most worthy of note in it that through the motion of the equator, which is the measure of time, there is an immediate entrance from the ninth house into the eighth, which is the house of temporary death, as man understands that he must be living in God down to his temporary death, so that between that and his life in God, no part of time may intervene.

The **Second Triplicity** is that of the MC angle, which they call the tenth house; and it pertains to youth; and it is called the triplicity of *action*, and of *profit* or the Worldly Good emerging from it; if indeed doing everything physically, on account of *physical good* it does its own thing for itself. For, as by the motion of the equator or the *Primum Mobile* it moves from the ASC angle to the MC angle, so does man progress from boyhood to youth, and from *being* or *life* to *acting*; but the other two houses of this triplicity are the sixth and the second.

Moreover, *profit* or *physical good* emerging from the man's own actions is a threefold thing. **First** in the order of dignity and nobility it is immaterial, as are arts, rulerships, dignities, and honors, to which man is raised up because of his well-deserved merit, famous actions, and capability. Whence there are kings, and magnates who sell dignities and honors to sin against nature. Therefore, of this triplicity, the angle of the MC lays claim to be the principal house.

The **second** is [the house of] animate material things, which are subordinates, servants, and animals; and it is located in the sixth

---

[1]That is, in the clockwise direction.

house, following [the MC] in this triplicity according to the motion of the equator.

And finally, the **third** is [the house of] inanimate material things, such as gold, silver, equipment, and the other goods that are also immobile, acquired by his own labor, which things are attributed to the second house under the name of *riches*. This whole triplicity, therefore, is one of *action* or *art*, then of the good things emerging from it.

The **Third Triplicity** is the one of the DSC angle, which they name the seventh house, and it pertains to *virility*; and it is called the triplicity of *marriage* or *love*. For as by the motion of the equator from the angle of the MC, the progress is to the angle of the DSC, so from youth to virility, and from famous actions to marriage and to friendships with men, which are united by that, and these are sought because of an innate desire for perpetuity, for it is not sufficient for man to [enjoy] good and beautiful living alone; and therefore, since a living creature is sociable by nature, he seeks out a congenial association for himself in which he finds pleasure; for such is also given in divine things, by which the universal happiness of divinity would bring down the elevated things. But now, his association is not with inferiors, such as servants, nor with superiors, such as masters, but with equals in the same degree of society.

But the other two houses of this triplicity are the third and the eleventh. Moreover, a man is joined together with another in three ways: the first connection in order of dignity and nobility is a bodily one, which they call matrimony—the primary cause of attaining perpetuity; and therefore, the principal house of this triplicity is said to be the DSC angle. The second is [a connection] by blood, which comprises brothers and relatives in the third house, which follows in this triplicity according to the motion of the equator. Finally, the third is one of simple benevolence, from which are born friends in the eleventh house. This whole triplicity is therefore one of *marriage* and *love*.

Finally, the **Fourth Triplicity** is the one of the middle of a dark night, or the IMC, which they say is the fourth house and the pit of the planets; and it is attributed to old age; and it is called the triplicity of *suffering*. And the other two houses of this triplicity are the twelfth and the eighth.

Moreover, the *first suffering* of the Native by the order of nature is that which he received at the beginning of life from his parents, as from the producing causes; in effect, every Native has himself both as one suffering and as an effect; but his parents, as acting and effecting causes; first, moreover, the suffering effect is from an effecting cause. Not only does the Native suffer from his parents in his body, but also in his mind on account of the blot of Original Sin, which his parents imprint upon his mind through their seed or flesh. Therefore, the parents and their status during the life of the Native, and then those things good and evil that are to be hoped for him have their own significations in this house.

The Native's *second suffering* consists of all of those *afflictions* of his body—namely, *illness, imprisonment, exile, servitude*, and the other things that he suffers during his life; and therefore, all these things and their causes, as *enemies of life*, are attributed to the twelfth house under just one category of enemy, which hence must rightly and truly be said to be the valley of miseries, and which follows in this triplicity according to the motion of the equator.

Finally, the *last suffering* of the Native pertains to the eighth house and consists of his *death*, which the Native suffers at the end of his life; and because death, is[15] the end of temporary life and the beginning of eternal life; therefore, according to the second motion, or that of the planets, which is from the setting to the rising, from the eighth house there is an entrance into the ninth, which is [the house] of life in God, as man may understand for himself through the second motion of living, which is attributed to the

---

[1]Reading *sit* 'is' instead of *seu* 'or'.

mind or the reason (as the first and rapid motion is attributed to the body, or to the sensory desire) must be crossed over from temporary death to life in God, which is life everlasting.

Therefore, in these triplicities, that which is *first* in the order of nature or dignity always occupies the nobler houses, namely the *angular* ones, because second are those *succedent* houses according to the motion of the equator, and because *last* are the *cadent* houses, which are also coming next [in order] according to the motion of the ecliptic or the planets.

Therefore, from what was just said, the Native's life is threefold. In itself, in God, and in his children; and these are of his true lives, not moreover his metaphorical ones, for the Native does truly live in God and in his children; and there cannot be any more. By the same logic, his profit or Worldly goods are threefold—immaterial, animate material, and inanimate material; and there can be no more. In the same way, the bodily connection is threefold: by body, by blood, and by simple benevolence; and no more are given.

Finally, the Native's suffering is threefold: at the beginning of life, during life, and at the end of life; and nothing beyond that is given in this World.

Therefore, nothing can be happening to a man that does not pertain to some one of these twelve houses. This is also worthy of note: that from the ASC angle the Native is seen as a solitary individual, from the DSC angle as an associated person, by the MC angle as an acting person, and by the IMC angle as a suffering person; and man's contemplation is directed towards these four [conditions], as is well-known to every wise person.

Finally, it is worthy of note that the cusps of the twelve houses are attributed to the subjects of human life, just as these are analogues to the first motion around the horizon; for the circle of position of the rising point or the one destined for life would not signify life if the *Caelum* did not ascend from that part above the horizon.

Chapter 6. *Things that Must be Particularly Noted about the*
Significations of the Houses.

Now I ask, who will think that this division is absolutely fictitious or fortuitous, with the twelve domiciles of the *Caelum* seen to
be in such an outstanding concord and marvelous order by
triplicities? Or that such concordances in things so abstruse and in-
termingled are accustomed to concur by chance?

This division, therefore, is natural and one drawing its origin
and arrangement from infinite wisdom, and embracing all those
mundane things (at least generically) that can be asked about concerning a man, seeing that the knowledge is the same, and that can
be asked about a thing pertaining to any house, affirmative or neg-
ative, and also contrary.

As for example, since a man knows by the force of natural light
that there is one God who made this World and who governs it, as
was shown by us in Book One, and who must consequently be
very greatly worshipped and loved, as the trine aspect of perfect
friendship teaches by the first principles of the nature of all things,
because of the inclination of the first house into the ninth house,
which is [the house] of religion.

From the stars and planets occupying those houses by body, by
rulership, or by aspect, judgment is made as to whether the Native
will be inclined toward the worship of God and to religion, or in
truth to irreligion; then about other things that pertain to that subject. Similarly, from the seventh house the conjecture is made
whether he is going to lead a married life or rather a celibate life.
From the fifth, whether he is going to have offspring or not? And
so with the rest of the houses.

Moreover, the contrary things signified by the houses are disclosed thus. For example, since the seventh house is the principal
house of the amorous triplicity of marriage, namely because it is
angular, and therefore it claims for itself the amorous connection
of the body and public matrimony, so on the contrary it signifies

public bodily divorces, or open enemies, and hence lawsuits, duels, and those things that follow them; and the reasoning is the same for the rest [of the houses].

Furthermore, this light from the triplicities quite clearly distinguishes that which pertains to each house per se, and it discloses the errors of those who make judgments from houses that are alien to the matter in question. For example, almost all the astrologers, following Ptolemy, have falsely thought up till now that illnesses pertain to the 6th house per se, although per se they pertain to the 12th house, which is [the house] of bodily afflictions and especially the essential house of illnesses from the division proposed above; however, the 6th house is the house of servants and animals per se, but in addition to the essential signification of the houses, there is this property of them in addition, that any house signifies the same thing but weaker as that to which it is opposed, on account of that opposition, and because both of them are included in the same circles divided crosswise.

And thus the sixth house by accident, or secondarily, signifies illnesses, imprisonment, and secret enemies, by reason of the opposition; and in turn, the twelfth house by accident bears the signification of servants and animals. Similarly, the seventh will by accident be a significator of illnesses and death because it is opposed to the first, which is per se the significator of health and life; and in turn the latter will by accident signify marriages.

And for the same reason, astrologers indiscriminately judge about religion from the third, about riches from the eighth, about parents, and especially about the mother from the tenth, about children from the eleventh, although they do not realize the genuine cause of the truth of their judgments, since from their books, but especially from Ptolemy, it is permitted to conjecture that they were indeed deceived in that because the essential signification of each house was unknown to them, which only becomes known through the superior Cabala; although Hermes, convinced by experience, offers something similar in his Aphorism 42, when he says "the ruler of the second has the same force in impeding as the ruler of the eighth; similarly the ruler of the sixth has the same as the ruler of the twelfth."[1]

But they err more seriously who judge about things neither by their proper houses nor by the opposite houses, but by those that are absolutely alien to the signification, as if someone would judge by the twelfth about riches, or brothers, or the spouse, or children without any more valid cause than that Jupiter, Mercury, the Moon, or Venus is in the twelfth; but here in addition is detected the error of Ptolemy and his followers, who almost solely judge about individual things from the angles of the figure and the Lights and the relationship of the other planets to the angles and the Lights; for, as an example, the angle of the first house is the angle of life, but the Native's life is threefold—namely, in itself, in God, and in his children, about all of which they deny that judgment can be made solely from the angle of the first house. And so with the rest of the houses.

Chapter 7. *Questions raised by Pico Mirandola, Alexander de Angelis, Marsilio Ficino in his Plotinus, and by Other Haters of Astrology, in Opposition to the Astrological Houses with Refuting Answers.*

On account of the hitherto unknown superior Cabala it is plainly evident how easy and unrestricted it was for the haters of astrology to hiss at those houses, to attack [them] with laughter, then to uncivilly inquire why the *Caelum* should not be divided into more than twelve houses? Why the first house should be called the house of life and located in the east? Why the order and numerical succession of the houses is from the rising through the middle of the night into the setting? Why the second house is the

---

[1]Here is the translation from Hermes's *Centiloquy,* contained in the book by James Herschel Holden, *Five Medieval Astrologers* (Tempe, Az.: A.F.A., Inc., 2007), "The ruler of the 2nd has the same force for impeding as the ruler of the 8th. Similarly, the ruler of the 6th and the ruler of the 12th." This secondary signification of opposite houses is also mentioned by Rhetorius the Egyptian (early 6th century) in his astrological *Compendium.*

house of profit or of riches, but the twelfth is [the house] of enemies, imprisonment, and miseries? And finally, why the other houses are also called by their own names and are disposed in that order? Since both the order and the names of these houses seem to smack of not an order but rather a mere chimerical confusion and to be a mere fiction, and are in fact an inane laughing-stock and are plainly fictions, as Pico in his Book 10,[1] and Alexander de Angelis, in his Book 4, chapter 27,[2] twist themselves about in varied and wretched ways to prove this.

Moreover, I reply to the **first** [question] that the *Caelum* was divided into 12 houses and no more because each of the 4 parts of the Angles of the *Caelum*, which preside over birth, vigor, decline, and death, aspect two other Celestial parts of the same nature with them by trine; whence from each of the 4 cardinal angles there came forth three places of the same nature; moreover, three times 4 makes 12, neither more nor less.

To the **second**, I say the first house is called the *House of Life* for this reason, because man is said to arise in it first on the mundane scene when he takes the first breath of mundane life; and therefore, since the first spirit of mundane life is at his birth, it must be located in the rising [part], just like the rising of any other physical thing; for the rising of terrestrial things is moved forward by the rising of the celestial bodies. And as the rising degree of the *Caelum* emerges from the shadows into the light,[3] so is the cause of the rising and emerging of everything that is then being born; namely, because whatever emerges from itself is more conformable to the degree of the *Caelum* that is ascending from the lower World into this light of the World, as is set forth by us elsewhere.

---

[1]Mirandola, Giovanni II Pico della, Lord of, *Disputationes adversus astrologiam.* [Disputations Against Astrology] (Bologna: Benedictus Hectoris, 1496).

[2]Angelis, Alexander de, Father, *op. cit.*

[3]Cf. Paul of Alexandria, *Introduction*, Chapter 2, where he speaks of a sign rising *ek tou aphanous tou kosmou merous eis ton emphanê kosmou* 'from the invisible part of the cosmos into the visible part of the cosmos'.

To the **third**, I say that nothing refers to the celestial influxes or to making predictions, by what number the houses are called—second, third, or fourth, but only that the *Caelum* has four triplicities, as it is divided above, and that the nature of the houses may not be varied[1]; nevertheless, the *physical* order of the houses is from the *rising* through *noon* to *setting* according to the motion of the prime and most universal physical cause, to the parts of which succeeding each other according to that motion, the principal states or ages of things in general were above related to the equator, the principal circle of the prime cause, according to their own succession.

And so, *physically*, the House of Enemies is the second in [that] order, the House of Friends the third, the House of Rulership the fourth, and so on in order. But *mystically*, or by *analogy*, the *numerical* order was instituted from the rising through the IMC to the setting; and the reason for this is that there are two motions in the *Caelum*—the **first** and prime motion, which they call the *rapt motion*[2]; the **second** is that of the planets, which, not opposing the rapt motion by which it is moved around, but nevertheless [having] its own proper and orderly motions arranged in a region contrary to the first, follow their laws inviolably.[3]

I say too that there are [such] motions in man, who is called the *microcosm*. One is the appetite of the senses, which is a motion in man like that in the animals, and it is first in the order of nature and also impetuous; the other is the rational appetite, which motion is

---

[1]Morin means that the natures of the triplicities as he defined them above are natural for the reasons previously stated and cannot be changed.

[2]The word *rapt* means 'seized' or 'carried along', here referring to the supposed motion of the *Primum Mobile*, which carries the signs and planets along in a clockwise direction.

[3]In other words, there is a *physical* order of the houses that is due to the apparent rotation of the *Caelum*, and that is in the clockwise direction—1st house, 12th house, 11th house, 10th house, etc. But there is also a *mystical* or *analogous* order in the counter-clockwise direction—1st house, 2nd house, 3rd house, 4th house, etc. *Analogous*, because that is the order of motion of the planets through the signs of the zodiac; and in a *contrary region*, which is the ecliptic circle.

man's as a human being and contrary to the first motion, and then in itself very restrained.

But now, since of these motions of man the *first* one has the greater analogy with the motion of the *Primum Mobile*, and the *second* moreover with the motion of the planets; they have therefore judged that the *Caelum* ought to be divided for man according to the succession of the signs, or the direct motion of the planets, for they are sometimes retrograde or stationary, just as a rational appetite is sometimes retrograde or stationary in its own course, when it is seized or overruled by its sensory appetite.

But this is only done by an analogous consideration and not on account of any physical cause, as if a motion of the *Primum Mobile* should insert itself per se into the sensory appetite of man, and the motion of the planets per se into the *rational appetite*, since the planets are moved to some extent by their own motion, then by the [motion of] the *Primum Mobile* itself, they flow per se into the *sensory appetite*, or into man to the extent that he is an animal, even as into other animals and living things. But neither the planets nor the *Primum Mobile* per se flow into the *rational appetite*, or into man to the extent that he is rational, because of a reason not originated by a natural principle but by a supernatural one.

Nevertheless, in that mystical analogy many things very worthy of note can be perceived—doing no little for the salutary instruction of the mind—and among other things this especially, that the first cause looked at for the man being born and in his birth; that is, from the planet or the part of the *Caelum* occupying the ASC angle, two ways occur immediately—one of the *sensory appetite*, by which the motion of the *Primum Mobile* is transferred to that analogue by way of its ascension and superiority into the 12th house, which is [the house] of all the *miseries* of life.

And the other way is that of the *rational appetite*, by which the motion of the planets is conferred on that [other] analogue, [so that] by way of its descension and humility, man is brought down into the House of Goods or of Riches with its own virtues of possessions, namely the second house, from which it is made evident to that man which of these ways is the better one, and how it is safer for him to follow the motion of the *rational appetite* than that of the *sensory appetite*, and therein to be made humble rather than to be exalted.

Finally, I say to the **fourth** question: that the reason why each house should be called by its own name and not by any other is in the constitution, the distinction, and the explanation of the triplicities laid down above, which shines forth more clearly than the light of noon. Therefore, we are making an end to our conception of the celestial houses., which, even though it is plainly new and unheard of before us, it is nevertheless firmly based upon physical reasons, and, taking its origin from the loftiest things, it is reduced to them, aiming at this—that the invisible things of God from the creation of the World might be perceived through those things that were made understood.

Chapter 8. *Whether if Man had not Sinned, the Superior Division of the* Caelum *and the things Signified by the Individual Houses would have had a Place and Force in the Nature of things with Respect to Man.*

At the first glance, this question indeed seems to be a difficult one, especially on account of the 6th house, which is the [House] of Servants; the 10th, which is the [House] of Dignities; the 12th, which is the [House] of Illnesses and of the rest of the bodily afflictions; and then finally, the 8th, which is the [House] of Death. If indeed all of these things are supposed to be greatly alien to a most happy state of original innocence, and only introduced as a punishment for Sin. Whence, the revered Paul [says] in Romans, Chapter 5, "Death entered into the World through sin."[1] That man in his

---

[1]Romans, 5.12, *Propterea sicut per unum hominem peccatum in hunc mundum intravit, et per peccatum mors; et ita in omnes homines mors pertransivit...* 'Therefore, just as Sin entered into the World through [the action of] one man, and death through Sin; and so death passed into all men...'.

state of innocence is subject to the stars for these things seems to be very much opposed to the perfection of that state, as well as to the dignity of man.

Nevertheless, it must be brought forward, that even if Adam and his posterity had not sinned, the higher division of the *Caelum* would still have subsisted, and it would have been allotted its own effect on everyone born, to the extent that it would have been permitted to Nature or to the individual rulers of the sublunar World. Indeed, Adam himself—although he was not produced by the concourse of the stars, but supernaturally, would, at the moment in which he first drew a breath of air, have been made subject to celestial impressions, just as any other man who is now born of woman.

Moreover, this assertion is proved in three main ways. **First**, because after Adam's sin, the nature or virtue of the stars was not changed, as in fact some can suppose without reason or authority, absurdly dreaming that Adam's sin, or that God, because of his Sin, has overturned or perverted all of Nature; and that fire, for example, would not have been going to have the force of burning without Sin. Since, as the Sun now illuminates and heats, and indeed burns up [things], so also before Sin it would have been able to rule over the same things. And if those things are conceded about the light and heat of the Sun, they must be conceded all the more about the [astrological] influences, for those are the essential and specific properties of the stars; moreover, heat and light that are essential qualities of the stars, are common to fire and to many sublunar things, which are not distinguished specifically among themselves.

Add that on account of that Sin itself, the planets would have been despoiled at least of their fortunate influences, as would honey, wine, fruits, and other things eaten for the sake of their own pleasing flavors, flowers of their sweet odors, and in general, minerals, vegetables, and animals of their own characteristics, by which either as nourishments or as remedies they would have been

25

able to benefit man. Therefore, since it is proved by experience that all these things have endured, and therefore things of the sort that were made on account of man before Sin, so that, at least with the advent of Sin, man himself from the boundless goodness of God and from his own ingratitude would have been more confused and dissatisfied; [and since] it must scarcely be thought that any change was made in the celestial bodies on account of man's Sin, but from that Sin itself there followed the greatest deprivation and a great ruin solely in human nature. And it is not that the words of Genesis, Chapter 3, are opposing, where God says these things to Adam, *The Earth will be cursed because of your action; you will eat from it in labors for all the days of your life; it will produce thorns and thistles [for you], etc.,*[1] for this curse is not given to the Earth first and per se, but for the labor or work of Adam; for before his Sin it had produced thorns and thistles by itself, but not in places where it would have been cultivated by men, and this was for the particular privilege of man, whose work God everywhere had blessed; and similarly it must not be said that the terrestrial Paradise existed undisturbed by the influences of the stars; for, since the place on Earth in which Adam must have worked according to [Genesis], Chapter 2, was crammed full of fruit-bearing trees, for the maturation of which the Sun was necessary, and also the Moon, it is plain that that place was not lacking in influences made more powerful by that same heat. And finally, it was not neglecting the man in his state of innocence, because he would be exposed to the impressions of the stars, indeed of the elements, because Jesus Christ the Son of God, infinitely purer and more worthy than all men, did not wish His own body to be free from such impressions so long as He was a traveler [in this World], but He experienced cold, heat, and thirst.

Secondly, it is proved, for the virtues of that proper division and their individual effects existed in the state of innocence, with only

---

[1] Genesis, 3.17-18 ...*maledicta terra in opere tuo; in laboribus comedes ex ea cunctis diebus vitae tuae. Spinas et tribulos geminabit tibi...* '...cursed the ground in your work; you will eat of it in labors for all the days of your life. It will produce thorns and thistles for you...'

those excepted from which man would have been made exempt by the privilege of innocence and the good will of God, as it is shown in the several triplicities of the above division. If indeed the Triplicity of Life had existed unscathed—for man to have lived in himself, in God, and in his own children—indeed, [he would have lived] far more perfectly than in the state of fallen nature.

Similarly, the Triplicity of Marriage[1] would have been intact, for men would have contracted marriage, and they would have had brothers and sisters, and other relatives; then, friends bound by the tie of particular benevolence, which it can then [be seen] in Christ, who had particular inclinations of friendship for Master John the Evangelist and Lazarus; then, also by reason, for from Master Thomas, Part One, Question 96, Article 3,[2] necessarily in the state of innocence there would have been some disparity among men. For those things that are from God were ordained, Romans 13,[3] but the order was greatly in disorder according to Augustine.[4] Moreover, this disparity would have been: *First*, partly by sex, because generation would have been there, and partly by age. *Secondly*, partly by reason of the spirit for justice, knowledge, and free choice, since everyone would have been more or less able to apply himself to learning and working. *Thirdly*, partly by the body, by reason of a better complexion, or being more beautiful, or being stronger, etc., because the human body shares more or less either in that sort of influx from the *Caelum*, or in that sort of causes of Nature.

Having posed these things about the inequality of bodies and the minds resulting from the varied influx of the stars, as the Di-

---

[1]Houses 3, 7, and 11.

[2]St. Thomas Aquinas, Th.D. [c.1227-1274], *Summa Theologica* 'Theological Summary', Part 1, Question 96, "Of the Mastership Belonging to Man in the State of Innocence."

[3]In Romans 13, Paul says that every man should obey authority and be in subjection to it; and he should also love his fellow man and not commit crimes.

[4]In the section of the *Summa Theologica* previously cited, two statements from Augustine's *City of God* are cited.

27

vine Doctor rightly notes, there would in fact have been no risings of enmity, neither open nor secret, on account of the perfection of that state, but individual men would have been overtaken by mutual love; on the other hand, firm and true personal friendships would have been contracted, not only among like persons, because that is the first and most necessary foundation of friendship, but also among unlike persons, as in the same article Master Thomas vouches for it; for those who were eminent in virtues, the science, arts, or bodily skills, would not like today have been the object of the envy or hate of some, but rather of the love and benevolence of everyone, and a man endowed with a heroic temperament or uprightness, even though not devoted to the sciences, would have greatly esteemed a man eminent in knowledge, and vice versa; and therefore, the Triplicity of Union[1] would have been totally prolific in its own proper effects.

But now for the rest of the Triplicities there occurs an occasion for doubting, for if the Triplicity of Action[2] and the worldly good coming forth from it had existed in the state of innocence, from that it would seem to follow that some men were preferred to others, but the latter were put under the former, and both sets of them relied on acquiring riches for themselves, which would seem to be contrary to that very free state, and the one in which all things were in common.

Truly, it can be answered in two ways. *First*, that even if they would not have been preferred to or subject to any other persons, the Triplicity would still have been present, for, seen in its own simplicity, it is only [the Triplicity] of Action and Worldly Good, by the grace of which it works, because it is threefold—[ruling] immaterial things, sensitive material, and insensitive material things. Moreover, the 10th house is [the House] of those Actions and of immaterial Good, of which sort are profession and arts. But now in the state of innocence, man would have been much less free

---

[1]Houses 3, 7, and 11.
[2]Houses 2, 6, and 10.

than he is today, but he would [still] have acted with his body and mind in accordance with his proper nature; and so from the 10th the quality and success of his actions would have become known, then the arts and the rulership to which the man is disposed.

And because man will rule over the animals, vegetables, and minerals, in connection with these he would have worked for the sake of proper or common convenience; and since the fruit of his actions belonged to him rightly by nature; therefore, in raising animals, in cultivating the fruit-bearing trees, and the plants,[1] as well as household equipment made by art from metals, stones, woods, and then pictures and such like things, he could have abounded in them just as a proper ruler, with a true poverty of spirit, and with esteem towards his neighbor, and with not even a shadow of sordid avarice seen among men; for the [American] Indian forest dwellers, among whom the land is [held in] common, have generally followed this simple kind of life [following] the lead of nature.

And so, there would also have been good sensitive material and insensitive material, and consequently the whole Triplicity of Action and Worldly Good or profit. I reply secondly, since Master Thomas, who in general favors us in this matter, in Article 4, [says] that since man's condition in that state of innocence was not nobler than the condition of the angels, among whom some are superior to others, also among men there would have been some superior to others and ruling as far as rulership is referred to, and conceded rulership over good and joy, but not over evil and punishment of subordinates. Since the Divine Doctor says, "Man is naturally a social animal, but the social life of many cannot stand, unless someone who is at the head with the knowledge of the common good is strong and undertakes its care; and it would have been unsuitable, if those who excel in art, knowledge, and justice, would not have used them for the benefit of others."

To this I add that men in that state, especially praising and honoring God, and devoting their time to perfecting the sciences and

---

[1]Reading *plantis* 'plants' instead of *Planetis* 'planets'.

the liberal arts, and although none would then have been repro-
bates, as are born now on account of the judgment rendered to the
woman in Genesis 3[.16], *I will multiply your hardships and your
conceptions*; nevertheless, there would have been such a number
of predestined persons spread out over the face of the Earth, especially on account of the longevity of men, that in various regions
the most magnificent temples would have been constructed, and
there would have been men more suitable than others for presiding
over sacred things; and therefore very many men would have been
exalted to honors.

For neither craftiness, hypocrisy, gold, promises, arms, and
other nefarious arts would have raised some men to governorships
or princely status, intent only on suppressing their subordinates, so
that they might grow fat from such actions, or delivering them to
exile, prison, and not to fire,[1] so that they might be a terror to others; and those have the power to turn the divine and human laws
upside down with impunity for [their own] pleasure, having
scorned all reason of justice and virtue. But the splendor of virtue
and justice with public assent and joy would have advanced famous men to honors and rulership, who would have devoted themselves and their own things to the utility of their subordinates,
without any regard for their own convenience, [but] with the most
unrestricted love. Add that God himself would generally have chosen men dearer to Himself, whom He had entrusted to be in charge
of others in some thing. Are there not in the celestial hierarchy
some spirits in charge of others?

So, therefore, the Tenth House would not have been devoid of
governorship, or the signification of rulership; and because it is
equal and just that he who does not work for himself but rather for
others has in turn those who provide themselves with necessities;
and the allegiances of subordinates to him aside from servitude
and gifts would not have been lacking, not opposing the sharing of

---

[1]The Latin has *nec igne* 'and not to fire', but perhaps we should read *aut igne* 'or
to fire'.

goods, namely because it would have been pleasing to individuals to honor more worthy men with things occurring in more worthy things, in art, in culture, in education, or in invention.

And hence it would have happened that men preferred to others or of greater excellence would always have abounded in gifts, but would have been ready to pour them out on others; and so the Sixth House, which is [the House] of Subordinates, and also the Second, which is [the House] of Natural Goods, would have been made good by his own labor or by the merit of things made. And therefore this whole triplicity would have persisted intact.

There remains the last Triplicity—apparently more unbearable than the others in the state of innocence, that is the Triplicity of Suffering at the beginning of life, during life, and at the end of life, which embraces houses 4, 12, and 8. In fact, no one can doubt that at the beginning of life the Native would have suffered from his parents, just as the effects from their own efficient causes, since every effect, as such, has a kind of suffering, although this one does not have to continue very long.

But more seriously, sufferings crowd in during life and at the end of life. For Master Augustine in his *City of God*, Book 4, Chapter 10, and elsewhere, will have it that Adam would never have been going to suffer and [experience] evil if he had not fallen from the state of innocence through his mortal Sin; and Master Thomas, in his *[Summa Theologica]*, Part 1, Question 97, Articles 1 & 2, would have that man in the above said state to have been without suffering and immortal; and the reason for that is because if he had been capable of suffering, he would also have been corruptible and mortal. But from [the passage of] Master Paul cited above, *only through Sin did death enter into the World.*[1] In fact, it seems that here some things must be said in advance, some explained, and some distinguished.

---

[1]Morin is apparently paraphrasing Paul, Romans, 5. 12, *Sicut per unum hominem peccatum in hunc mundum intravit, et per peccatum mors...* 'Just as through one man Sin entered into this World, and through Sin, death...'

First, that man would not have been immortal by Nature, but only by the gift of Grace, as Master Thomas states in Article 1, and Master Augustine confirms in Book 9 [commenting on] the New and Old Testament, in Question 19, when he says, that man would have been immortal through the force given from heaven, which force was none other than that of the Tree of Life; whence that same Augustine says in his City of God, Book 14, Chapter 26, *There was food for man, so that he would not hunger, drink so that he would not thirst, and the Tree of Life lest old age should destroy him*; and this is entirely confirmed by Genesis, Chapter 3, where [it says], *God cast out Adam from the Paradise of Pleasure, and he placed Cherubim and a flaming sword revolving about to guard the way of the Tree of Life and he would eat and would live eternally.*[1] That is, his own strength, being weakened by age and the action of the elements, is renewed and restored by virtue of that Tree of Life as often as it was needed for him; therefore, man's body was not immortal by Nature, but by Grace, by which, lost through Sin, death entered into the World.

Second. That since man of himself was mortal, and only immortal through Grace, and finally by virtue of the beatific vision one per se incapable of suffering and immortal, he would have been translated to a spiritual life and per se one incapable of suffering and immortal, more quickly or more slowly, just as was pleasing to God, or man would have been excited more ardently by the love and desire of God.

---

[1] Genesis 3.22 *...nunc ergo ne forte mittat manum suam, et sumat etiam de ligno vitae, et comedat, et vivat in aeternum. 23. Et emisit eum Dominus Deus de paradiso voluptatis... 24. Eiecitque Adam, et collocavit ante paradisum voluptatis Cherubim, et flammeum gladium atque versatilem ad custodiendam viam ligni vitae.* '...now therefore, lest perchance he might put out his hand and also take [fruit] from the Tree of Life and eat it and live eternally. 23. And the Lord God sent him out from the Paradise of Pleasure... 24. ...And he ejected Adam, and he placed Cherubim before the Paradise of Pleasure and a flaming sword revolving about to guard the way of the Tree of Life'. In his citation of these chapters, Morin has rearranged the order of the statements ineptly; but perhaps we should read *ne comederet* 'lest he would eat' instead of *& comederet* 'and he would eat'.

Third, that man would have had neither hidden nor open enemies, nor would he have been exposed to prison, exile, servitude, hardships, and similar miseries and sufferings, which are the punishment of Sin; but also neither to illnesses, namely because illnesses happen to man now, not only on account of sins, especially of gluttony and luxury, but mostly on account of the ignorance of man himself; for now he knows neither his own internal dispositions nor the forces of external causes—that is of the elements and the stars—nor the future effects resulting from the concourse of both of those, nor imminent danger [occurring] by chance or accident; and therefore he frequently falls into illnesses, wounds, and death. But in the state of perfect nature, he would have known all these things very well and would prudently have avoided them; and therefore he would not have been seized by any illness, but he would not however have therefore existed incapable of suffering, or free from all suffering or [physical] alteration, which is most evidently proved by this—that is, because he would never have needed the Tree of Life to repair his natural strengths, and that Tree would have been unnecessary.

Add that such an incapability of suffering does not pertain to the state of Nature, either intact or in decline, but rather to the state of glory; and so, he would have suffered heat, cold, fatigue, hunger & thirst, just as other animals; and therefore now and then from the cooling of a river, or the shade of trees, or from a draft of cold water, or from the heat of the Sun or a fire, but more frequently he would have needed sleep, food, and drink, for he would not have drunk nor eaten unless he needed to, and he would have recognized his need without any sense of it, and therefore he would not have avoided that alteration of his body and the diminution of his strength by the celestial bodies and the elements, [but] in order to restore those things, he would return to the Tree of Life because it was man's supreme and Catholic medicine.

And the things said above are not for the punishment of Sin, since they accompany the nature of man; but the punishment of Sin is either to lack remedies suitable for those things or to be ignorant of those things that in his former state had never occurred and would therefore have always preserved him immune to illnesses. For this, temperance and strength—outstanding virtues—would have been in use among men, on account of the love of God and its close utility, which could not have been the case without both suffering and virtuous endurance.

From what was said, therefore, noting **first** and **second**, that the end of this life of man was established, and, having left aside the previous life, he was bound to pass into another life, and consequently to experience [suffering] at the end of this life, since such an exchange cannot be conceived without suffering; that change would however have been without the separation of body and mind that is properly called death, about which Master Paul speaks, but similar to the change that happened to Christ, when, without death, He was transfigured on Mount Tabor.[1]

Moreover, from the **second**, noting that it is known that He would also have suffered many things during this life; and if not those evils that now happen to men either on account of their own sin, or on account of the malice of others, or on account of ignorance, or on account of an accident, but if he would have voluntarily put his own hand in the fire, without doubt he would have burned himself, and he would not have been able to prevent that suffering by the virtue of his own mind, as Master Thomas opines in the above said Article 2, for that was beyond the nature of acting causes and suffering, otherwise he would never have needed the Tree of Life, but the virtue of mind alone would have provided [Him] eternal life. Consequently, the whole triplicity of suffering would have had a place in the state of innocence. And man, also from [the passage of] Master Thomas cited above, would not have been immune to the influx of the stars.

Moreover, that Adam, even though he was produced by God alone, would have been subject to the influx of the stars like the

---

[1] The transfiguration is mentioned in Mark 9: 2-3 and elsewhere.

rest of men, as we have asserted from the beginning, is established from this: because at the beginning of his life he suffered from God, so that it was made from his own cause, however all the other things would have been common to him with the other men. For since there would have been the same human nature, if the other men would have been exposed to the impressions of the elements and the stars, as we have shown above, why would Adam [too] not have been exposed to them? Or if he was free [from them], then why weren't the others free?

In fact, the difficulty is plainly resolved in Genesis: 3, if authority was needed in this matter. For the Tree of Life would not have been given free to Adam for any other end than that it would have repaired the damages to his constitution and his powers caused by the stars and the elements, and thus he would have kept himself immortal so long as it would have been pleasing to God; otherwise, the Tree of Life would have been unnecessary for him, as was already said above about other men.

From this, it is certainly especially confirmed that in the case of those who are born by the ordinary force of Nature, [their prospects] should not be judged astrologically from a celestial figure erected for the moment of conception, but rather for the moment of the nativity, in which that Native by his first inspiration of air receives the force of the celestial constitution, and in that way is impressed just like soft wax, and consequently a little retarding or acceleration of that same moment of nativity can procure good honors for him and avert great evils from him.

Someone may say that in fact the things said above are true about the sufferings of the body, but the principal difficulty resides in the depraved propensities of the mind towards gluttony, extravagance, anger, and the rest of those things to which from the influx of the stars men are now addicted, even as are the brute animals.

Besides, this is certain—that in that state of pure nature, men would have been different among themselves in form, temperament, and morals or natural propensities just as they are now—and Master Thomas cited above witnesses that. Besides, the influences of the stars are no different now than those that they had before the Sin, because it has not changed their nature, just as it has not changed that of the elements. But now "the same remaining the same always does the same on the same"; therefore, since human bodies and the stars ruling them would then have been the same as they are now, and the same propensities would also have been impressed by the stars on those being born as are impressed now—either good or evil. And that is plain from Eve, about whose sensual appetite it is said "The woman saw that it would be good to eat of the tree, and it was beautiful to the eyes and of a delectable appearance."[1] [which] also happened] before she made the decision and ate. Whence her propensity for gluttony is demonstrated, which was known to the Devil.

This would therefore have been the whole difference between the two states: that in the state of pure nature, sensuality would always have obeyed reason, while now it resists reason and more often overrules it; and Adam would have earned that for himself and his own posterity from divine Grace, if he would not have sinned. Nevertheless, it would have been necessary for everyone to fight it out with the Devil and with his own sensuality. Then, because neither Adam nor Eve nor the Lord Jesus himself was immune from that struggle, for when Christ was hungry he was tempted; then, because each one from something suitable ought to be promised eternal life, as much as would have been in him. Then finally, because the Devil with the permission granted to him would have left no man untested, even if he had prevailed with no one; but he would have tempted each one in those things to which he would have been more inclined by his nature.

From these things, it is plain how badly Junctinus explains his Objection 24 in his own defense of astrologers, when he objects to that one, that if Adam would never have sinned, there would not

---

[1]Genesis: 3. 6.

have been an eighth house, which is [the House] of Death, since the stars now have the same influence as they had before Adam's sin. For he answers with the Master of Judgments in the 4th Discourse, Chapter 48, and with other theologians, "The *Caelum* is not now of virtue equal to what it was in the beginning of creation, and the light of the Sun and the Moon, and of the other stars, was struck and diminished by the Sin of the first man, before which [time] the stars shone seven times more brightly than they shine now," which are pure suppositions, agreeing with no place in Scripture and with no physical reason.

With due respect I would have said of those theologians, whose authority on physics [made] without any reason, I judge to be not creditable, since the theologians are either spurning or more lazily straining out accurate knowledge of physical things, especially celestial ones; and treating of those things for the most part, they frequently make absurd mistakes, and those are taken as principles for false dogmas of theology, as can be seen here and there in the books of the Scholastics. Therefore, much that relates to scholastic theology must not be admitted, unless [it is by] one who properly knows physical things, or at least theologians of the kind who probe deeply into physical things before they undertake to enlighten others. And let this be my warning about theologians.

Section II.
The Erection of Celestial Figures for Astrology.

Chapter 1. *Six of the Astrological Houses are Above the Earth and Six Below.*

Since in Book 14 we followed the natural lead of dividing the *Caelum* into twelve domiciles, so now [we follow it] for the division of the same *Caelum* into astrological houses, and the prime divisions of that same Nature would have to be observed by us and followed, lest we should err and only hand down to posterity chimerical and false or doubtful things in place of true and certain ones in the manner of the ancients; indeed, the [opinion of] the ancients in this matter—the principal and fundamental one of all astrology—is so far so sluggishly emerging, that hitherto there has been a controversy about the manner in which Ptolemy erected a figure, and this is explained differently by different persons.

First, therefore, among all things it now usually suits astrologers—with Ptolemy agreeing in *Quadripartite*, Book 3, Chapter 10—that 6 of the astrological houses are above the horizon and 6 below; with which opinion [they agree], even if they oppose the ancients, those who follow the Equal House System, dividing the *Caelum* by circles through the poles of the ecliptic and drawn across the twelve parts of the zodiac[1]; and then, Alchabitius [d.c. 967] and [John] of Saxony and their followers, dividing the same *Caelum* by circles passing through the poles of the equator,[2] whence from the latter and the former the individual houses are partly above and partly below the horizon, except when the pole of the equator for the latter, but for the former the pole of the ecliptic, happens to be found on the horizon; however, Nature herself has not yet put an end to this daily quarrel among all astrologers, as was rightly known.

Therefore, Nature first divides the space of the World and the whole *Caelum* into two equal parts by the great circle that they call the horizon or the surveyor, and some of them appear entirely above the Earth, and also all of the others lie hidden under the Earth. And this first division is very apparent, and at length it causes a difference of virtue with respect to the Earth and its inhabitants, so that as long as the stars remain under our horizon, they do not affect us at all, at least by their own elemental qualities, as is plain from the Sun, which having fallen under the Earth, does not heat us, but is weaker in its influentials than when it is above the horizon, because of the interposition of the Earth,

---

[1]This system divides the zodiac into 30° sections beginning with the ASC degree.

[2]This is the so-called Alchabitius system of house division, which was popular during the middle ages and in general use prior to the publication of the tables of Regiomontanus houses in 1490.

38

whose dense solidity often blunts the otherwise unrestricted force of its influence.

Furthermore, if after that general division of Nature, the space of the World or the *Caelum* must be divided into houses with respect to man, it is known from the *Cabala of the Houses*[1] that some parts of the *Caelum* ought to rise for that man, some ought to culminate, and others ought to set. But where there is no meridian, there is no part of the *Caelum* that rises, culminates, or sets, nor is there given any rising or setting, or any point from which the beginning of a division can rightly be taken, as happens under the pole of the equator.[2]

Therefore, for dividing the space of the World or the *Caelum* into astrological houses, the circle of the horizon is not sufficient, but to be sure a meridian is also required, passed through the poles of the equator and the horizon distant from each other one way or another; and now these two circles divide the whole *Caelum* into four equal quadrants, of which two are above the Earth and two below the Earth, then there are two rising and two setting, differing both in their location, and in their virtue; for it is from the four circles of the sphere—the ecliptic, the equator, the horizon, and the meridian—in which the principle force of the *Caelum* shines forth; the first two because they are purely celestial (against the opinion of the Copernicans), with a purely celestial and most universal virtue; that is, they lay claim to no particular place on Earth.

But in the case of the latter two, because they cannot be conceived without [both] the *Caelum* and the Earth, but each of them joins together, by which a most efficacious force is discovered, which is born from the connection of the *Caelum* with a particular

---

[1] A reference to Morin's book, *Astrologicarum domorum cabala detecta a Joanne Baptista Morino* (Paris: J. Moreau, 1623) 'The Cabala of the Astrological Houses Discovered by Jean Baptiste Morin'.

[2] Only partly true. At the north pole, the meridian is obviously arbitrary, since it can be drawn in any direction to the equator. However, there is a definite rising and setting. The ASC is always 0 Libra and the DSC is always 0 Aries.

place on Earth. Therefore, Nature herself proclaims that the former must be intended for use in dividing the *Caelum* with respect to particular places on Earth, and she indeed evidently manifests their powers in those places, as JoFrancus Offusius, who wrote against astrology, always greatly admired the virtues of the stars and their effect in rising, setting, in the MC and the IMC, but he had frankly confessed he was ignorant of their cause.

Therefore, the four hemicycles of these two circles, including the four previously mentioned spaces are so distinguished in their powers, that the one that is in the east presides over the rising of things, the one in the MC over their vigor, the one in the setting over their decline, and the one in the IMC over their demise; and that is universally [true] of all things that are of a corruptible kind, as is said in the Cabala mentioned above.

Therefore, with the *Caelum* divided thus into four quadrants out of necessity by those two circles, of which two are above the Earth and two below, entirely as Nature indicates, because by the subdivision of it into smaller parts for man, for whom besides those general [rulerships], many others are also characteristic, such as dignities, religion, servants, etc., they should be joined together by the subdivision of those same quadrants by circles by the intersections of the horizon and meridian.

Then, because Nature most plainly displays that same division and its way through those points, and not through any others, but then especially because if it should be done through other points, then there will either be no virtue of those circles in the figure, which cannot be said, since both by the authority of astrologers and by daily experience before the rest it may be judged to be the greatest, or there will be given in that same figure two other fictitious circles, falsely usurping the name and the virtue of the horizon and the meridian, which will be absurd, or of greater virtue, which will be [even] more absurd, or finally equal [in virtue], which would be superfluous.

Therefore, the *Caelum* or the Mundane Space must not be divided into twelve houses by points other than those that Nature herself indicated to us by the intersections of the meridian and the horizon everywhere on Earth. But having agreed on this, there will always be six above the horizon and the same number below; therefore, the truth that was proposed at the beginning of the chapter is established.[1]

Moreover, from this, two things follow among others that must be considered here. *First*, that in those places on Earth exactly located under the pole of the World, either nothing is born, because there is no rising or setting of the *Caelum* there,[2] and consequently there can be no rising, vigor, decline, and demise of anything, or, if anything is born there, it is necessarily monstrous or irregular and spurious because the influences there are entirely confounded.[3]

Second, because those who live under the equator enjoy the virtues and influences of the whole *Caelum* because for them the whole *Caelum* rises and sets, [but] under the pole only one half of the *Caelum* is perpetually above the horizon, the rest is always hidden; finally, those who live in the oblique sphere have themselves in a middle mode, but they share the fate more of its end, and also of its site.

But from this it is the case that under the equator the generations of every kind of animal, vegetable, or mineral can be made, but none can be made under the poles, or only spurious and monstrous ones. But in the oblique sphere, the closer they come to the equator, the more generations there are, and the closer they are to the

---

[1]Here Morin declares that the only true method of house division is based upon the subdivision of the equator, which is the method of Regiomontanus, familiarly called "the Rational System."

[2]Not so! For there is a rising and setting, as mentioned in an earlier note.

[3]Polar bears may be born there, but Morin would have called them 'monstrous'. Marie Peary, daughter of the polar explorer Robert E. Peary, was born 12 Sep 1893 at 6:45 PM on Greenland near 78N25 74W00. (I do not know what time zone Peary's watch was set to.)

poles, the fewer there are[1]—namely, just as more or less of the *Caelum* ascends over the horizon.

But having explained these things thus, it must certainly be seen by what scheme the division of the *Caelum* or the Mundane Space should be brought to completion. If indeed about this matter diverse systems are found by astronomers, no one has hitherto put and end to a controversy of such moment. For even though we have stated above that a subdivision must be joined together by circles passed through a section of the horizon and the meridian, nevertheless it must be taught in addition by what scheme this ought to be done, and [also] that other methods must be rejected.

Chapter 2. *In which the Equal House System of Dividing the* Caelum *into the Astrological Houses is Subjected to a Particular Examination and Rejected.*

Among the various methods handed down by the ancients for the division of the *Caelum* into the astrological houses, it seems to us that this one must be particularly examined, because it was particularly cultivated by the ancients down to our times, so that Cardan strove to demonstrate the truth of astrology by 100 nativities erected in that system, and there are still some who, having scorned the truly Rational System of Regiomontanus, think that the Equal House System[2] should be adhered to.[3]

Moreover, it is called *Equal* because it divides the ecliptic and therefore the whole *Caelum* into 12 equal parts by circles drawn through the poles of the ecliptic itself, having taken its beginning from that point on the ecliptic which is found rising on the horizon

---

[1]Apparently a reference to the fact that there is a greater diversity of species in lower latitudes than in higher ones.

[2]Here and below Morin simply speaks of "the Equal system," but I have added the word "House" to that to make it plainer for the reader.

[3]Morin's contemporary, Nicolas de Bourdin, the Marquess of Villennes, favored the Equal House System, as did the 20th century English astrologers Charles E. O. Carter (1887-1968), and Margaret E. Hone (1892-1969) who adopted it and taught it in her books and classes.

at the moment of time when the figure of the *Caelum* is erected. Moreover, that this system is alien to the truth and must be rejected is proved by the reasons set below, not yet previously duly considered or set forth.

First. Because each house is on the contrary divided by the horizon, so that one part of the individual [houses] is above and another below the horizon, with only the exception of a unique case, namely when the pole of the ecliptic happens to be found on the intersection of the horizon and the meridian; but from [what is said in] Chapter 1, no house is divided thus, but each one must be wholly above or below the horizon, lest it be deprived of the nature of the individual houses by a two-fold site. Add that Ptolemy would have his *apheta*[1] to be in a house above the Earth and not in one below, with the exception of the first house; and if the individual houses were to be partly above and partly below the Earth, what a great amount of calculation would be required to determine the portion of each house that is above and that is below the Earth!

Second. Because logic, experience, and the consensus of astrologers prove that the beginning of each house is the most powerful point in that house, or the most effective, and then that the force and property of that house is continuously slackened, so that in the last 5 degrees it is scarcely observable and rather inclines to the nature of the following house; and consequently, in the Equal House System the beginning of the tenth house ought to be that way for actions, rulership, and dignities, but which in fact experience proves to be false, so that the followers of that system have always been driven to note the point of the ecliptic that is situated in the middle or in the Heart of the *Caelum*, as if it is the most valid for those significations, and to judge from it, and to direct it, although in that same Equal House System it frequently happens that such a point is the beginning of the eleventh house, to which such significations scarcely belong—namely, because the beginning of the

---

[1]The *apheta* (Greek for 'starter') is the starting point for the primary direction relating to the length of life. It is also sometimes called the *hyleg*.

tenth house does not fall in the MC, but short of it or beyond it, except when the beginning of Aries or of Libra is ascending.

Moreover, the degree beginning the tenth house in the Equal House System is not accustomed to be directed by the supporters of that system, with the exception of the cardinal points of the zodiac. But already if this absurdity occurs for the beginning of the tenth, it will therefore occur proportionately for the middle and the end. And similarly for the other individual houses, with only the sole exception of the beginning of the first house or the ASC; for if the supporters of the Equal House System observe the Heart of the *Caelum* or the cusp of the tenth according to the Rational System,[1] why should not the same thing be done for the rest of the houses?

And if the degree of the ASC is effective in directions, why is it ineffective for the degree of the tenth in the Equal House System, but [rather] recourse must be had to the degree of the MC? Thus, therefore, this division destroys itself and overturns the true locations of the planets, and it absolutely produces unreliable [prognostications]. And it is not contradictory that now and then it provides true prognostications, since there is no system of dividing the *Caelum* that is so erroneous that it does not sometimes have the planets in the same kind of house as the true and Rational System; and consequently can concur in prognosis with the same by reason of what is signified by that house.[2]

It is proved in the **third** place, because beyond the Arctic Circle, a figure cannot be erected according to that system when the ecliptic coincides with the horizon, which always happens somewhere in the frigid zones. For a valid reason combined with experi-

---

[1]That is, the Regiomontanus House System; but of course the same argument would hold for the Campanus or Placidus System, since the MC degree is the same for all three of them.

[2]Here he says that if the Equal House system occasionally puts planets in the same houses as the Rational (Regiomontanus) system that does not prove anything. However, advocates of the Equal House system cite examples where that system puts planets in different houses and puts different signs on the cusps of houses that seem to be satisfactory. And the same would be true in some cases with the placement in still other systems. So Morin's argument is not conclusive.

ence may be given, why one degree of the ecliptic rather than another may be taken for the ASC degree.[1]

Besides, that the Equal House system is erroneous is proved much more evidently by experience with natal figures, among which we may only choose some in which that error is made most manifest.

XIX

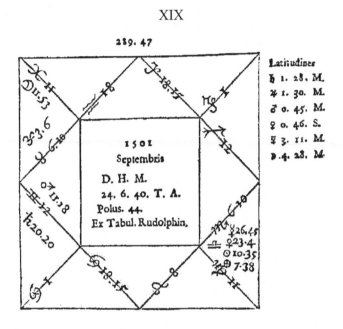

Jerome Cardan
Padova 45N24 11E53
214 September 1501 6:40 PM[2]

---

[1]This argument is entirely false! There is always an ASC degree at and above the Arctic Circle and even at the north pole itself, where the ASC, regardless of the time, is 0 Libra. Consequently, it would always be possible to erect a horoscope according to the Equal House System in any latitude. But Morin's favorite, the Rational system, like all the other quadrant systems, fails above the Arctic Circle.

[2]This chart is the 19th Example Horoscope in the book cited in the next note. It is not included in Morin's text, but I have added it for the convenience of the reader. Note that it is drawn in the Equal House System, and that in the 9th house the Cor Caeli, or "Heart of the *Caelum*" appears at 18°46 Capricorn.

First will be that of Cardan, the Prince of Astrologers, who also in his *Book of 100 Nativities*[1] asserted that he had worked more than thirty years on that. Moreover, it happened for Cardan that previously and for a long time he had refined the above said Equal House system, as is plain from that *Book of 100 Nativities* erected according to that system, among which is also found this figure, plainly with the same ASC degree, but the Moon is found in the 11th house, which begins at 6° 10' Pisces; therefore, the Moon in the 11th house was determined by virtue of that location to causing and signifying friends according to [our] Book 21, Section 2, and because Jupiter by reason of its rulership and its sextile aspect was determined to the same thing, and it was in the ASC; moreover, the Moon was in sextile to the ASC and Jupiter, both of which she was ruling by exaltation.[2]

Many and useful friends were signified by this, and especially women friends on account of the Moon and Jupiter being in feminine signs, and these women friends of great authority because of the Moon. But none of these things happened to Cardan, as is plain from his own judgment of his own nativity, entitled "On Friends and Enemies," the individual parts of which it would be too tedious to rebut, and from the point of view of our doctrine, it would be unnecessary.

For me, of course, it suffices to assume from that judgment of his own case that notwithstanding what was said above about the location, the rulership, and the aspect of the Moon and Jupiter, he bewails the small number, the contempt, and the disloyalty of his friends, and the abundance of secret and hostile enemies, to whose slanders and accusations he was exposed; and he does not cite any benevolence of magnates [and] ladies, but only that of two illustri-

[1]Cardan's *De exemplis centum geniturarum* 'Examples of 100 Nativities' (Nürnberg: Johannes Petreius, 1547); I have used the reprint of the 1662 omnibus edition of Cardan's works.

[2]But Morin neglects to note that while the Moon has a weak sextile to Jupiter, the Moon is in partile square to Mars in the 2nd house, which is an evil aspect for both friends and money, and Mars is ruler of the 12th house of secret enemies, so the Equal House indications were actually more bad than good.

ous Scots after the 47th year of his life on account of some particular affinity of their nativities.

And so, since the superior placement of Jupiter and the Moon was promising very many friends and benefactors, therefore, either astrological truth has collapsed, or the Moon must not have been in the beginning of the 11th house, nor was Jupiter the ruler of the 11th, and so neither of them was the significator of friendships; but rather, the Moon ought to be in the beginning of the 12th, so that it would strongly cause and signify very serious illnesses, secret enemies, and the many other great evils that he testifies that he had experienced.

Moreover, that this is the case is proved by Cardan himself at the end of [his translation of] the *Quadripartite*, where, finally having changed from the Equal House opinion, and explaining twelve nativities[1] erected according to the Rational System, and his own among the others, the figure of which is put here,[2] [but] with the planets' places now calculated from the *Rudolphine Tables*, he found that the Moon is not in the 11th house, which is the house of friends, but rather in the 12th, namely the house of illnesses, secret enemies, and in short of every misery and bodily suffering which the Native experiences during his life. And Jupiter is not the ruler of the 11th but rather of the 12th, and consequently it is not the significator of friends, but of enemies and illnesses. And this figure, or the division of the *Caelum* into twelve houses, squares with Cardan's accidents.

---

[1]Here, Morin refers to Cardan's book, *Liber XII geniturarum* 'The Book of Twelve Nativities'. Most of the charts have Regiomontanus cusps, but Cardan's does not.

[2]Morin's figure, shown next, has Regiomontanus cusps, while Cardan's figure actually has Alchabitius cusps, and in it the Moon is still in the 11th house, but the 12th house cusp is 29 Pisces, so, as in the Regiomontanus system, the 12th house is ruled by Jupiter, although its joint ruler would be Mars.

The Nativity of Jerome Cardan.[1]

289. 47

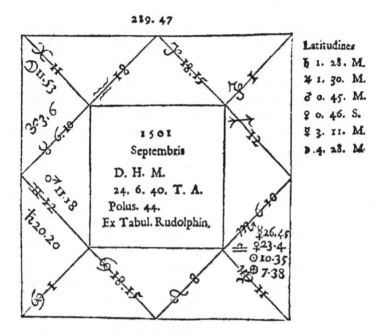

Latitudines
♄ 1. 28. M.
♃ 1. 30. M.
♂ 0. 45. M.
♀ 0. 46. S.
☿ 3. 11. M.
☽ .4. 28. M.

1501
Septembris

D. H. M.
24. 6. 40. T. A.
Polus. 44.
Ex Tabul. Rudolphin.

Padua 44 N
24 September 1501 6:40 PM
[Note that in the list of Latitudes,
the Latin M means South and S means North]

For first the Moon is found here to be the ruler of the 4th, which however it was not in the Equal House mode; and so it is the significator of the parents, but especially of the mother on account of its own nature and the feminine sign that it occupies; therefore, since it is in the 12th house and powerful in the ASC, but afflicted by the almost partile square to Mars, also with Jupiter ruler of the 12th and taking possession of the 8th, the reason is evidently plain

---

[1] As recalculated by Morin with Regiomontanus houses and planetary positions from the *Rudolphine Tables*. (But the actual latitude of Padua is 45N24.)

why he experienced a huge danger to his life partly from his mother at the beginning of his life, when he was violently extracted from her womb as if he were dead.

But then in his first months he was seized by the plague and then by dropsy, for which accidents Cardan offers no cause, since however they would have happened again from the afflicted Moon. For Saturn's square is in nearly the same circle of position with the Moon on account of the south latitude of the Moon itself, and therefore this was very unfortunate for the square of the malefics; and in the first months it came by direction to the square of Saturn, according to Cardan's figure, but not in the eighth year, as he himself though, on account of the neglected latitude of the Moon. And since the Sun in the 6th is also a significator of illnesses, by its annual motion it arrived at the Moon's place in the month of February next after the nativity, [and] it was badly afflicted by the squares of Saturn and Mars conjoined to it around the 11th degree of Gemini; and therefore this was the time of those illnesses; but dysentery [leading] to death down to the completed seventh year was from the direction of Mars to the ruler of the 12th and by the direction of the opposition to the eighth to the body of Saturn, of which the arc is 7°26, but not from the direction of the Moon to the square of Saturn, as Cardan was thinking.

Moreover the two cases of a tertian [fever] in the year 1528 was from the direction of the ASC to Mars, as Cardan will also have it, and the flow of urine that was of terrible and stupendous duration happened from the direction of the ASC to Saturn. Therefore, Cardan's celestial chart does not square with the Equal House System, but rather with the Rational System, as is plain from what was said above.

After Cardan's nativity, it seems that ours ought to be added, because both the *Caelum* is disposed in almost the same manner, and because both his and ours [were charts of] a physician and an astrologer, and one born to achieving fame from his writings. Moreover,

This nativity is outstanding among the others and famous for its evils, on account of that outstanding concourse of planets in the Vale of Miseries, that is, in the 12th house according to the Rational System; moreover, all [the planets] with the exception of Mars, have come together in the 12th house of the figure of the New Moon that was celebrated on the day before my own nativity, as is plain in the first figure that is put below, which is also outstanding from the Pleiades in the ASC, and with the constellation of Cygnus in its zenith, then with the Eye of Taurus in the 1st and the heart of Scorpio in the 7th.

The Figure of the New Moon Preceding
the Nativity of Jean Baptiste Morin

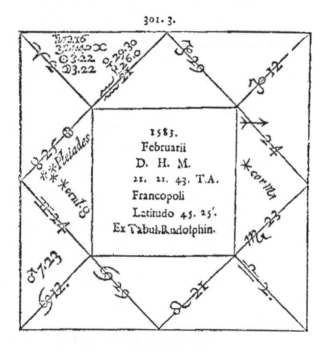

22 February 1583 9:43 A.M.
Villefranche 45N25

[The longitudes in the 11th house are not clear in this reproduction. They are ♄ 12)(16, ♃ 4)(40, ☉ 3)(22, ☽ 3)(22, Venus 29≈30, and Mercury 26≈00. And in the 1st house we see ocul.♉ The Eye of Taurus' (Aldebaran), and in the 7th house cor ♏ 'The Heart of Scorpio' (Antares).]

The Nativity of Jean Baptiste Morin.

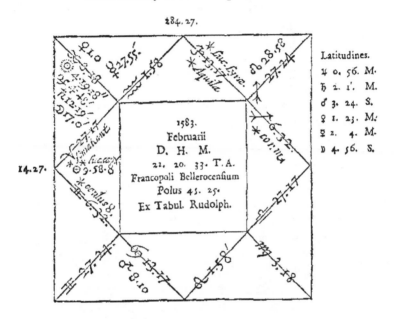

22 February 1583 8:33 A.M.
Villefranche, Beaujolais 45N25

Nevertheless, this figure also has many outstanding features that ought to be discussed more opportunely, and a wonderful tempering from the benefic nature of Jupiter and Venus [rulers] of the 12th house, and of the Lights that are posited in that house. For when the benefics are the causes and significators of evils, these are either lighter, or if they are great, they [come] at least with the hope of remedy or of avoidance, which very frequently happens, as is also plain from Cardan's nativity; and it will be said here and

51

there in its own place in this work about the good and evil [influences] of this nativity, in order to display the truth of astrology.

Here, it will be sufficient for us to show by this figure, exactly rectified by many notable accidents, how greatly the Equal House System is alien to the truth.[1] For the cusp of the 12th [in my chart] would have been 27ℋ34, and the cusp of the 11th would have been 27♒34; and so all those planets would have come together in the 11th house, which is the House of Friends, and Mercury would have been on the cusp of that 11th house.

Oh, Me!—thrice and four times [would I have been] blessed, if the division of the *Caelum* according to the Equal House System would have been true and natural, since if planets can signify in any way, the way that is most powerful is by bodily position, whence [comes] that common axiom among astrologers that the presence of a planet can do more than the rulership of one that is absent.

Good God! How many male and female friends, kings, princes, and ecclesiastical magnates I would have had, and all of them useful benefactors, on account of the Sun, Moon, Jupiter, and Mercury strong in that house, with the Moon only conjoined to Saturn, ruler of the cusp of the 11th, which it could not harm! And how few the enemies if I had been able to pass through life without any of them! What freedom of life would have happened for me! How many good things on account of Venus and Mercury, rulers of the 2nd house, conjoined to Jupiter, and how few evils!

Finally, what good fortune [would have occurred] for my parents after my birth, on account of the Sun and the Moon, rulers of the 4th; and yet I have experienced a more frightful fate. For first, around my twelfth year, in which the Part of Fortune had come by direction to the square of Mercury, ruler of the 3rd, it happened that with my father and mother fatally ill, she from child birth from

---

[1]Here, and in what follows, Morin makes a strong argument against the validity of the Equal House System of house division.

which she died, he from a fever from which he escaped, my elder brother asking me in a childish way, whether if one of the parents was going to die, which one would I think it would be better to die? Simply and in my own ingenuous manner, it seemed to me that it would be better for my father to survive, as it turned out, however, loving both parents equally, and more strongly my mother.

Moreover, from that day on, until the two following, during which she died, she incurred such a hatred for me (whom she had always deservedly loved), that she would neither give anything to me in making her will, nor would she bestow her own blessing on me before her demise, if she had not been strongly warned by relatives and priests unless about the nullity of the will and the danger to her soul. Finally, she blessed me prostrated as I was with grief and weeping and stupefied about the cause that was not known to me, and she made a legacy as small as she could, and she gave three tines that much to the youngest of my sisters, but she appointed my brother [her principal] heir, and at the end she very religiously fell asleep in the Lord.

Moreover, the reason for this is very evident, because the Moon, ruler of the 4th and the Part of Fortune, and consequently from its own nature the ruler of the mother, and signifying fortunes, is found in the 12th with Saturn, which was portending for me hatred and loss of fortune from my mother; and that (as I afterwards thought) was because of my brother, who perhaps reported my answer to her. For that direction of the Part of Fortune to the square of Mercury, significator of brothers, was indicating that.

With regard to that, a common axiom among astrologers is this: As many imprisonments are signified as there are planets in the 12th house; and it was scarcely lacking in my youth that it would have been verified, because of the passions of vindication and lust arising from Mars and Venus ruling the 1st house, and indeed a great evil (that perhaps would have turned out more seriously), not withstanding Saturn in the 12th, was thwarted and prohibited by the benefic nature of Jupiter and Venus, rulers of the 12th conjoined in the 12th, and that now and then with a dangerous but most fortunate outcome, on account of which I gave humble thanks to Divine Goodness, and I continue to give thanks as often as it comes to mind.

Moreover, because that cluster of planets in the 12th house with Saturn ruler of the MC could not cause imprisonments, it did cause servitude, for servitude (as in being shut up in a fortress) is a certain kind of incarceration, because man is not free in another's house, but held in bondage to another person. Since from my 16th to my 46th year, my life was one of perpetual servitude, and I had 16 masters, all of whom I abandoned, either on account of quarrels with the mistresses of the house, since I couldn't tolerate their commands, [and thereby] I experienced their hatred, on account of the Moon and Venus in the 12th, which brought me many evils, losses, and dangers to my life from women; or on account of sudden occurrences; or on account of the unbearable ingratitude of my masters; and some of them were commoners, on account of the Moon and Saturn, such as notaries, administrators, secretaries; others were middle-class, such as directors, abbots, bishops, and others who are magnates of the royal court on account of the Sun, such as a certain Duke,[1] whose Ordinary Physician I was through nine years in the time of the French War Against the Heretics, about whom it can scarcely be said how much I had obtained, since for his life and fortune I had three times fallen into danger of violent death, and I would have been most happy to have dared as much for him, because no other physician would have tried,[2] and whom at last I was forced to abandon on account of his very great ingratitude, predicting a fatal illness for him within two years before I departed, from which he also died.

---

[1]Jean Hieroz, in his book *Ma Vie Devant les Astres* (Nice: Éditions des Cahiers Astrologiques, 1943) identifies him as François de Bonne, the Duke of Lesdiguières (1543-1626). His chart is used for an example in Section II, Chapter 4, below, and in several other places in the *Astrologia Gallica*.

[2]The Latin text is translated as above. However Hieroz renders it as, *This last in particular, even though I had succeeded [in performing] on him an operation, and one that no other physician would have dared to attempt.*

But then I successively renounced all servitude with such hatred that I declined that of one Cardinal, and one Duke Marshall of France, and the top official of the Treasury, very fine men and benefic to me. And it must be carefully noted that from the years of my age from 21 to 37, at which time the direction of my ASC passed successively through the squares to Mercury, Venus, Jupiter, Saturn, and the Moon posited in the 12th house, it can scarcely be said how many miseries, illnesses, losses, misfortunes, and dangers to my life I would have experienced, from which however I escaped, through God's pity.

But already, would anyone who is an astrologer, unless he is weak in mind, offer the explanation that those things had happened to me from the Lights and the benefics in the 11th house, especially with them ruling the 1st and aspecting the Part of Fortune by sextile? Is there anyone who on the contrary would assert that these things would have been caused and signified by those same planets in the 12th, and especially by Saturn, who as the ruler of the MC in the 12th was portending servitude for me and greedy, ungrateful masters and damages, as will be demonstrated more evidently in its own place.

Besides, although in the figure of the New Moon, all the planets had come together in the 11th house, which is the house of friends, and therefore I would have become known to kings, queens, princes, cardinals, and primates of the kingdom; however, with the particular fate of my nativity prevailing, so far I have only come upon four or five persons with prime authority, probity, intelligence, and especially noted in science, who esteemed me either on account of my noble character or fellow feeling, and would have benefited me not as much as they would have wished, but as much as was permitted to them through the badness of fortune, the perpetual partner of my fate.

But from the year in which from a student I was made a Doctor of Medicine,[1] my memory shudders to recall what enemies I had,

---

[1] Morin received his M.D. degree from the University of Aix-en-Provence on 9 May 1613.

either on account of envy or on account of dislike, who tried to harm me in everything, and at least they harmed me in fortune, because from occasional good things with [overall] good fortune removed I had only trouble in fame and life, even though to inflict injury on anyone was always most distant from my nature.

And yet I acquired a perpetual antipathy to criminals, scoundrels, and those idlers endowed with a diabolical malice, who began to hate me even at the first glance, so that I in turn at the first glance recognized and hated their nature. Either the stars, or demons, or universal Nature might move a fantasy in this matter, which will be spoken of elsewhere.

But I also experienced envy and injuries from learned men, many of whom, from first being friends, were finally made enemies for me, with whom from the year 1635 to the year 1654 I waged war strongly and gloriously in defense of truth and my reputation, on account of Saturn's and Mercury's rulership in the 12th afflicted in the ASC;[1] but [also on account of] Mars, ruler of the ASC, in trine to that cluster of planets and especially of the Lights.

And it must not be passed over in silence that when in the year 1635 I brought forth into the light the Science of Longitudes invented by me, at which time the Sun had come by direction to the MC; previously, a notable astrologer of Avignon had predicted honors, dignities, and riches for me on account of the conjunction of Jupiter and the Sun, to whom I wrote back that such a direction doubtless presages fame, but also it portends the secret hatred of some Ecclesiastical Magnate and injuries from him rather than a dignity or something useful, on account of the Sun and Jupiter being in the 12th with Saturn, the ruler of the MC, which certainly how true it was—more truly it sprang from Cardinal Richelieu [1585-1642], after his iniquity perpetrated against me.

---

[1]This is not altogether clear. Saturn is in the 12th, and Mercury is in Aquarius, ruled by Saturn, but 5°23 above the cusp of the 12th in the 11th house. Saturn would be in its fall in the ASC sign Aries, but Mercury is in partile sextile to the ASC.

But that cluster of ten planets caused so many enmities and evils in the 12th house, not in the 11th house, and especially Saturn, ruler of the MC, the 7th, and the 11th, as is plain from the principles of this science most manifestly set forth by us.

Finally, civil wars, rapine, plagues, debt, law suits, and other evils that occurred from the time of my nativity reduced my parents to such a state of poverty, that they were not able to give me assistance in my studies, and also from my tenderest years it forced me to be the maker of my own fortune, just as necessity urged me on, and opportunity from studies was generally encountering other things also, since I neglected my studies for a decade. But in my nativity the Moon, ruler of the 4th, in the 7th with Saturn was evidently portending the future misery of my parents, with Mars afflicted around the cusp of the 4th, from which it was only distant by a perpendicular arc of $4°57'$.

Consequently, this nativity is shown to be greatly unsuited to the Equal House System, but greatly conformable to the Rational System.

But lest I may seem to want to establish my opinion on the nativities of only two astrologers, devoted to the science of the *Caelum*, we may now publish the nativities of men of a different profession—that is, kings and magnates, who covet the rulership of the Earth and the greatest honors of this lower World. And so here is presented the nativity of the magnanimous and very brave Gustavus Adolphus [1594-1632], King of Sweden, who was in those times a terror to all of Europe, and who in two years subjugated two-thirds of all of Germany with astonishing swiftness and ease, and whose violent death I predicted to Cardinal Richelieu, when he asked for my judgment on that matter four months before it happened—not in fact on the very time when it happened, but a little later on account of the false moment of his birth hour that was given to me and nevertheless taken for the truth, which was only able to deceive me, not in the type of the accident, but only in its time.

In that nativity, therefore, the MC according to the Equal House System would have been 6°26' ♍, and the cusp of the 9th would have been 6°26' ♌; and so Venus would have been inimical to the 10th house, and Saturn would not have been in the 8th, nor would the Sun have been ruler of the 8th; consequently, neither would have been the significator of death. But now if anything occurs in this nativity that is worthy of admiration, it is the very great facility of acting on death, about which it must be judged from the 10th house and its ruler. And yet neither is Virgo on the 10th, nor from Mercury its ruler, nor from that planet's state, nor from Saturn, ruler of Mercury, badly afflicted, nor from the benefics that were inimical to the 10th, nor from the aspects of the planets to the 10th nor to its ruler, can [his death] be sought in any way, as is well-known. Therefore, 6°26' ♍ does not suit the 10th house. Although for this, Saturn and Mars in the Equal House System would have afflicted Jupiter, ruler of the ASC and the lights, and yet that was not sufficient for a violent death because the ASC, the Sun, and the Moon were free from malefics, and neither of the malefics was determined to death, and not the Sun itself, but Saturn was in the 9th and Jupiter in the 3rd, but he died a violent and illustrious death while fighting; therefore, neither his life nor his death square with the Equal House System. Truly, if for the time transmitted to me from Germany, but having added five minutes to that hour, the figure erected according to the Rational System produces that which is discerned here and is conformable to the whole life of the king, his death and fame; and it depicts that exactly.

For first the Sun and the Heart of Scorpio[1] in the 1st, as well as the Eye of Taurus[2] in the 7th, and then Jupiter, ruler of the ASC, the Moon and the Sun in square to Mars, besides Spica Virginis[3] in the MC, and Venus, ruler of the MC, aspecting it by trine and conjunct Jupiter, ruler of the ASC and the Sun, were promising the greatest good fortune and such as he experienced in his undertak-

---

[1] The Heart of Scorpio is the star α Scorpii or Antares; it was in 4°07' Sagittarius.

[2] The Eye of Taurus is the star α Tauri or Aldebaran; it was in 4°08' Gemini.

[3] The star Spica or α Virginis was in 18°12' Libra.

The Nativity of Gustavus Adolphus, King of Sweden.

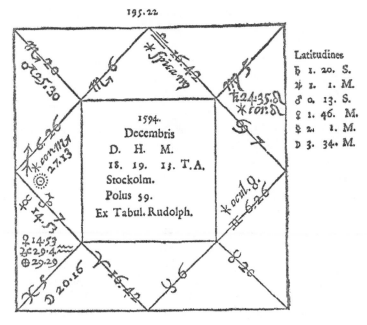

Stockholm, Sweden 59 N
19 December 1594 7:13 A.M.

ings and actions. Moreover, Venus and Jupiter with Mercury in the 2nd in evil aspect to Saturn and Mars promised huge works done by his own effort, but with bad skill and indeed violently done. But all the same, the Sun, ruler of the 8th, in the 1st, and Jupiter, ruler of the ASC and the Sun and the 8th,[1] in the 2nd afflicted by the nearly partile opposition of Saturn,[2] afflicted in the 8th, and also square Mars from the 12th house, were portending a violent death,

---

[1]The 8th house cusp is in Cancer, which is Jupiter's exaltation, so Morin takes it as a ruler of the 8th house, perhaps considering that the Moon, ruler of the cusp, was in Pisces, which is ruled by Jupiter. But this seems a bit strained.

[2]The longitude of Jupiter shown in the chart is wrong. It was actually in 24°09′ ♒. The typesetter evidently read 24.9 ♒ but inadvertently set it as 29.4 ♒. So it was partile square Saturn as Morin says.

which signification was supported by the Heart of Scorpio in the ASC and the Eye of Taurus on the cusp of the 7th, fixed stars that are first of the name of the very violent, and the Heart of Leo[1] with Saturn in the 8th.

Therefore, at the time when the MC was coming by direction to the square of Jupiter and Saturn, immediately and as closely following with the body of Mars afflicted in the MC. They were signifying the greatest misfortune in undertakings and battles and also a violent death, as I had predicted, which happened on the day of November 16, 1632, at the Battle of Lützen against Walstein [1583-1634], the Generalissimo of the Imperial Army.[2] And that occurrence of three anaeretas[3] was horrendous! Since the occurrence of the square to Jupiter, ruler of the ASC, which preceded it, was very bad because Jupiter was exalted in the 8th, and it was peregrine in a violent sign and very badly afflicted by malefics, and its ruler Saturn was afflicted in the 8th. Moreover, a public and famous death was being signified on account of the Sun, ruler of the 8th, in the 1st; and the death was from a fired piece of lead on account of Saturn in the fire sign Leo, and then from iron on account of Mars. If in fact he was also dead more times by the sword, a king so struck down, and as if more times he was slain, as [it says] in Virgil, where Evander boasts about Herilus in these verses:

And I sent King Herilus to Tartarus with this right hand,
To whom at birth his mother Feronia, horrible to say,
Had given three lives; and thrice moving arms,
Thrice he was sent to Lethe.[4]

---

[1]The Heart of Leo is the star á Leonis or Regulus; it was in 24°12′ Leo in close conjunction with Saturn.

[2]Albert von Waldstein, the Duke of Friedland & Mecklenburg and Prince of Sagan, also suffered a violent death just two years later as Morin explains below.

[3]The *anaereta* (Greek for 'destroyer'), sometimes spelled *anareta*, is the planet or point at the end of a primary direction that signifies death. Here, Morin says that any one of the three could have signified death.

[4]Virgil, *Aeneid* VIII,110 ff.

Where this also should be noted: that the direction of the MC to Mars in Scorpio was promising a victory, but an unlucky one, indeed a lethal one, on account of Mars badly afflicted by Saturn and inimical to the 10th.

And it must be carefully noted that in the annual revolution Saturn had come to the radical place of Mars, and Mars had come to the radical place of Saturn; but on the very day of his death, Jupiter was in opposition to the radical Mars, Mars was applying to the radical place of the Sun, and the Sun was precisely on the radical place of Mars; consequently, here again are present the same causes as above, but [we shall speak] more fully about these elsewhere.

Therefore, they are already sufficient to show how outstandingly the Rational System squares with experiences, but the Equal House System does not, according to which Venus would neither have been the ruler of the 10th cusp and in trine to it, nor would Saturn have been in the 8th, nor would the Sun and Jupiter have been rulers of the 8th; and finally, not at any time would an appropriate direction for death have occurred, all of which however were being required for the good fortune of this king terminated by a violent death.

Perhaps someone might object that death must not be judged from the direction of the MC, but rather of the ASC, or at least of a primary apheta. But I reply that that is indeed true for a natural death which resulted from illness. But in the case of a violent death, which comes about not from illness but from an action, such as a battle, a siege, or some other undertaking, very rightly from the astrological principles there is sought from a direction of the MC a judgment on the success of the action, which generally is the violent death of that Native, either from enemies, or judges, or from some other cause, or from a wound, imprisonment, or other things similar to those; and that was proved by many other examples.

But from what was said above, it is most evident how necessary astrological science is for kings, more so than for others, since it would be so easy to predict an imminent misfortune for a king. But God, who hardened the heart of Pharaoh, generally blinds kings, like this one, who entered into battle unarmed, and He does not give prophets to them, or astrologers warned by science, who would warn about imminent danger from fate, whence it happens that walking through the pathway of fate like blind men they fall into a pit; but [we shall speak] more fully about these things elsewhere.

To the nativity of the King of Sweden, it seems not without reason that the nativity of the Duke of Montmorency, Marshal of France, should be added, on account of the great affinity of the nativities and the accidents, so that from those things the truth of astrology may more clearly become known. For the same signs were in the ASC and the MC for both of them, and also the same royal fixed stars. Indeed, for both of them Jupiter and Venus, rulers of the ASC and MC, were conjunct, and these planets were signifying men who were famous, strong, warlike, high-born, generous, liberal, and fortunate in their actions, which they were down to the time of their violent death; but for both of them, both Lights were rulers of the 8th, and Saturn was afflicted in the 8th, which signified for both of them a violent death and a public one on account of the Lights.

Moreover, the King of Sweden died during a battle, and that was a glorious thing for him, at least in the presence of men, because the Lights were not afflicted by the malefic rays of Saturn, and the Sun was in the 1st house making a glorious name. But the Duke of Montmorency, even though he had been stabbed in battle with many wounds, on the 1st day of September 1632 at 3½ hours after noon, nevertheless did not die, but was captured on account of the Moon afflicted on the cusp of the 12th and on its own antiscion; and finally, accused of the crime of lèse majesté because he had waged war against his own king, his head was struck off amid the very great sorrow of all; and he died very piously and nobly, on account of Jupiter, ruler of the ASC, with Venus, ruler of the 9th, well disposed in the 3rd; if indeed in his nativity both

Lights were afflicted by the malefic rays of Saturn, that is with the Moon opposite and the Sun square and in antiscion, therefore a mean and ignominious death was being signified by those [aspects], for a man's fame is greatly subject to the state of the Lights, either in life or in death, when they are, as in this nativity, significators of death.

Moreover, he perished from the direction of the MC to the square of Saturn, on account of a battle that was rashly and unfortunately undertaken, like the King of Sweden himself, for the latter was not armed, and the former had entered the battle unaccompanied; and therefore their deaths were caused by their own actions, at about the same time, and Mars was portending the end of good fortune for both of them, because in this nativity it is opposed to the Part of Fortune, and in the nativity of the King of Sweden it is square the Part of Fortune. Marvelous, therefore, is the concordance of both nativities and their accidents.

But already it is plain that this figure erected according to the Rational System greatly squares with experience, but according to the Equal House System it does not square with experience, for 13 Virgo would have been the cusp of the 10th, which presides over actions, undertakings, and honors, and so Mercury would have been the significator of these, but Mercury is retrograde under the Sun beams, and very badly afflicted by the square of Saturn; therefore, with these [positions] it could not cause any good fortune in actions and dignities of the sort that happened to the Native, especially in naval battles, and all the less because Mercury [if it were] in the ASC and in the place of Jupiter, ruler of the ASC, would be in exile and fall, and mutually it is departing from Jupiter itself[1].

Moreover, if as in the Rational System [the MC] is put at 10°49′ Libra[2] with Spica Virginis in the 10th house,[3] it is imme-

---

[1]Mercury is retrograde, so it is actually separating from a sextile to Jupiter.
[2]Reading 10°49 instead of 1°49′ ♎.
[3]Spica was at 18°12′ Libra; and Cor Leonis or Regulus was at 24°12 Leo.

63

diately plain that Venus, the ruler of the MC and the Sun, posited in her own exaltation and conjoined to Jupiter, ruler of the ASC and Mars in Pisces, is the very evident cause of the above said good fortune.

The Nativity of the Duke of Montmorency.

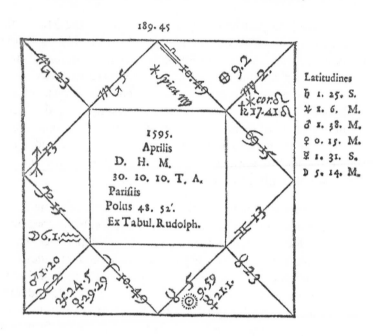

Paris, France 48 N 52
30 April 1595 10:10 P.M.

Besides, in the Equal House System 13 Leo would be the cusp of the 9th house, and so Saturn would not be in the 8th as significator of death, nor at the time of death would it give any cause or conformable direction; because the malefics are not accustomed to kill, when occurring either by body or by aspect, unless they were determined to death. But in the Rational System, where Saturn is in the 8th and the Sun is ruler of the 8th, the cause is very manifest. And so, the Equal House System must be entirely rejected.

Moreover, that the causes of death mentioned above are genuine is plain from the annual revolution, in which Mars was occupying the radical place of Saturn, and it was afflicting the Sun and Venus by square; moreover, Saturn was in the 12th radical house, which is the House of Prisons; then on the very day of his death, 30 October 1632, since Jupiter and Saturn, the significators of life and death, were opposed from the 6th and the 12th of the radix, and the Moon, ruler of the 8th, was with the violent fixed star the Eye of Taurus on the cusp of the 7th, and Mars, ruler of the 12th, was with the Heart of Scorpio, another violent fixed star, applying to the ASC and opposite the Moon; the Sun, ruler of the 8th , and Saturn were in their own opposition, conjunct Venus, ruler of the radical MC, which configuration was on all points very bad and violent, especially on account of the location and state of Mars and the Moon.

Moreover, on the day on which he was wounded and captured, the Moon, ruler of the 8th, was in opposition to the MC; the Sun, also ruler of the 8th, was on the Part of Fortune but square the ASC, Saturn was partilely on the cusp of the 12th, Jupiter, ruler of the ASC, was on the place of Mercury, ruler of the 7th, square the place of Saturn, and Mercury was in opposition to Jupiter, and Venus, ruler of the MC, was afflicted in the 9th and opposite the radical Mars.

Finally, we are adding the nativity of Albert, the Duke of Friedland & Sagan, Prince of the Vandals, commonly called Walstein,[1] the Supreme Commander of the Imperial Armies of

[1]He was Albert Wenzel Eusebius von Waldstein (1583-1634), commonly called in English 'Wallenstein', who became the Duke of Friedland & Mecklenburg and Prince of Sagan. He was an accomplished military tactician, who used his great wealth to send supply trains along with his troops instead of having them pillage the countryside for food and drink as they went along, which was the common practice. This enabled his forces to move more rapidly, which gave them a distinct military advantage.

Emperor Ferdinand II [1578-1637], who on the scene of this World was also no ordinary personage, [fighting] against whom the King of Sweden died in battle; and who was finally murdered at Galasius by order of the Emperor.[1]

Moreover, this nativity was sent to me from Germany along with that of the King of Sweden shown above; and I predicted a violent death for both of them from the directions of the MC to the square of the malefics in the 8th in exile, for such [positions] were fatal to the commanders of armies and to the rest of those undertaking battles or duels. And although Walstein did not die in battle, he was nevertheless slain by order of the Emperor—not without cause[2]—it was due to the fact that he had either not performed his own duty rightly, or that he had plotted some crime, on account of which he was destroyed; and so death came about from an action or dignity, which things the MC rules.

Furthermore, if this nativity is erected according to the Rational System, it is plain why he was raised up to more eminent dignities. For that was being signified by Saturn, ruler of the ASC, conjoined to Jupiter, ruler of the MC, in the 1st house, and trine Venus, ruler of the Sun, which, since it is made ruler of the 7th in the 7th, aspecting the Part of Fortune by trine, was presaging an illustrious fortune from military dignities, and Mercury, ruler of the Part of Fortune, in the 7th and in his own throne, and the Heart of Leo[3] on the cusp of the 7th.

Indeed, in the year 1631, in which he was opposed to the King of Sweden, he was elected Supreme Commander of the Imperial

---

[1]He was murdered in cold blood in his bed at Eger (now Chub, Czechoslovakia) by an English soldier in the employ of Emperor Ferdinand.

[2]Wallenstein, who had led the Imperial forces for some time, became disenchanted with Imperial politics and had begun negotiations with the leaders of the Protestant forces that he had previously opposed. The Emperor, the political head of the Catholics, viewed this as treason and offered a reward to anyone who would kill Wallenstein. Morin, being a good Catholic, evidently felt that the Emperor was justified in ordering Wallenstein's murder.

[3]Regulus, which was in 24°03' Leo

The Nativity of Albert Wallenstein, Duke of Friedland

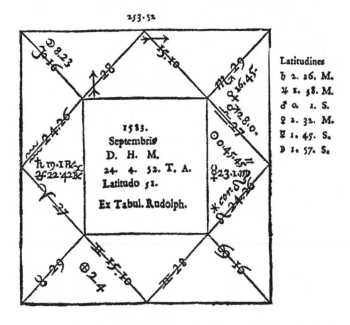

Czechoslovakia 51 N
24 September 1583 4:52 PM

Armies—the Sun had come by direction to the MC; moreover, a violent death was signified, especially from Saturn, ruler of the 8th,[1] in the 1st; and then Venus and Mars, rulers of the 1st,[2] in exile in the 8th, with the lights in violent signs.[3] Likewise, from bad po-

---

[1] Since Libra is on the cusp of the 8th and it is Saturn's exaltation, Morin takes Saturn to be the ruler of the 8th rather than Venus (or Mars, since Scorpio occupies most of the 8th).

[2] Again Morin chooses Venus to be a ruler of the 1st because Venus's exaltation sign Pisces is intercepted in the 1st; and he also chooses Mars to be a ruler of the 1st because most of the sign Aries is at the bottom of the 1st. But these rulerships appear to be chosen rather arbitrarily.

[3] Morin had no way of knowing that there were planets beyond Saturn. But it should be noted here that Wallenstein had Uranus closely conjunct the ASC degree retrograding in 23°51' Aquarius. We moderns can certainly see the influence of Uranus on Wallenstein's personality and career as well as his sudden demise.

sitions and also from squares from violent signs; therefore, from the direction of the MC to the square of Mars, he perished in a violent death, as I had predicted.

But if the figure had been erected according to the Equal House System, the cusp of the 10th would have been 24°26' Scorpio, and the cusp of the 9th would have been 24°26' Libra; and so the true and efficacious causes of his dignities would not have been given, because Mars, ruler of the 10th, in exile in the 9th, neither connected by a conformable aspect to the ruler of the ASC nor to the Sun, would not have signified those things; nor would there have been given true and efficacious causes of a violent death at the time of that death, because Mercury would have been the ruler of the 8th in the 8th, which would rather avert a violent death, since those malefic planets also in the domiciles of malefics[1] would temper their evils being posited in their own dignities.

Moreover, that the causes of dignity and death assigned above are true is plain from the day of his death, which was 25 February 1634. Since Saturn and Jupiter, which were conjoined in his nativity, at the hour of his death were opposed from the 10th and 4th radical houses, and square to their own radical place. Moreover, Mars the killer was retrograde on the place of Mercury and in the 7th house, and it was therefore opposed to the radical places of Jupiter and Saturn; and the Sun was separating from the antiscion of Mars, and Venus, ruler of the 8th, was applying to the radical ASC, and therefore all the above said causes were bad.[2]

But it is sufficient to have shown in five true and not at all common nativities that the Equal House System does not agree with experience, and the Rational System must be put way ahead of it. The same thing must be understood about another Equal System, which can be made by circles of declinations, dividing the equator

---

[1]Saturn is in its own domicile Aquarius, but Mars is in the exaltation of Saturn.

[2]The planetary positions on that date were as follows: Sun 7 Pisces, Venus 20 Aquarius, Mars 26 Virgo, Jupiter 22 Gemini, Saturn 21 Sagittarius, and Uranus 4 Libra.

into 12 equal parts, with the beginning taken from the horizon and the meridian.

Chapter 3. *Some Other Erroneous Systems of Dividing the* Caelum *by the Ecliptic or by the Use of the Degree of the Ecliptic that Occupies the Horizon.*

It is certainly marvelous and disgraceful among the princes of astrology that even though in some manner there is a unique mode of nature for acting, and therefore there can only be a unique natural system of dividing the *Caelum* into houses, on which alone the true principles of this science depends, yet they apply those principles indiscriminately to the divided *Caelum*, as is seen in their books, not perceiving that at the same moment of time by a figure erected in a different way, the locations and rulerships of the planets in the houses of the figure are altered in the individual systems. Therefore, it is of great importance that the true system of [house] division may be known, which hitherto has been settled more slowly than is proper.

Furthermore, among the rest of the systems of erroneous [house] division, the first is that of Porphyry,[1] which divides the two eastern arcs of the ecliptic intercepted between the rising point of the horizon and the meridian circle, above and below the Earth singly into three equal parts, and through the points of the division traces circles of latitude from the poles of the ecliptic; and so it has six oriental houses, to which are opposed the occidental ones; but this system is erroneous.

First, because this division is merely an artificial one without any natural foundation, by which it might be signified that the circles of the houses are from the moveable poles, or from traced points, having abandoned that fixed point of the division begun

---

[1]Porphyry was a famous 3rd century philosopher, to whom is attributed an *Introduction to Ptolemy's Tetrabiblos*, written about 295 A.D. In Chapter 43 he explains the house division system now called by his name, although it was explained a century earlier by Vettius Valens, *Anthology* iii.2 and attributed to an otherwise unknown astrologer, Orion.

from Nature and indicated in the intersection of the horizon and the meridian. Finally, the individual houses are partly above the Earth and partly below, as in the Equal House System, to which this is very similar. But the Equal House System, making a mistake with these causes also, is very much alien to experience, as was made plain above. Finally [again] , beyond the polar circles, when the ecliptic does not intersect the horizon, it will not be able to be put into use; it is therefore erroneous and only fictitious. [1]

The second is that of Alchabitius, [2] which finds the semidiurnal and seminocturnal arcs of the degree of the ecliptic that is ascending, and cuts both of them into three equal parts. Finally, through the points of the divisions and the rising degree of the ecliptic, having passed circle of declinations through the poles of the World, these circles in the equator denote the six right ascensions of the rising houses, which, having found the corresponding points of the ecliptic in a table of right ascensions, these houses become evident on the ecliptic.

Truly, this [house] division, which is also plainly fictitious, is without any natural foundation, and it makes houses that are partly above and partly below the Earth, and cannot be made use of when the ecliptic does not intersect the horizon. And here incidentally it must be noted that John of Royas in his astrolabe, after Alphonso and John of Saxony, the commentator on Alchabitius, [3] attributed

---

[1] But Morin's favorite, the Rational System, and all the other quadrant modes of house division also fail in the polar regions, so this argument is invalid.

[2] The Alchabitius System is so-called because it first became familiar to medieval astrologers in the 10th century astrologer Alchabitius's book *Isagogicus ad stellarum magisteria* 'Introduction to the Instructions of the Stars'. However, it was explained with an example horoscope of 428 A.D. by Rhetorius the Egyptian in his *Compendium of Astrology*, written about 505 A.D, but that book was unknown until modern times.

[3] Morin is perhaps referring to the translation of Alchabitius's books, *Praeclarum opus ad scrutanda stellarum magisteria isagogicum restitutum ab Antonio de Fantis qui notabilem eiusdem autoris libellum de planetarum coniunctionibus nusquam antea impressum addidit, cum Joannis de Saxonia commentario* (Venice: M. Sessa et P. de Ravanis, 1521. 4to) 'The Very Famous Work for Probing into *The Introduction to the Instructions of the Stars*, edited by Antonio de Fantis,

this system to Ptolemy, but wrongly, since Ptolemy separates the houses above the Earth from those below, and in Book 3, chapter 10, where [he speaks] about the prorogatory place, he asserts that the ASC is seen by a sextile aspect from the 11th house, by a square from the MC, and by a trine from the 9th, which does not happen in this method, [so] either degrees of the ecliptic are in aspect, as happens in the Equal House system, or degrees of the equator are in aspect. Moreover, it happens in the Rational System, having looked at the degrees of the equator or the proper ascensions of the individual houses.

But Ptolemy did not disclose his own mind more openly in this matter, and so he offered to posterity an opportunity for quarrels.[1] Moreover, the falsity of this method is very evident in my nativity, for I would have had all the planets, with the exception of Mars, in the 11th house—that is, the 12th [cusp] would have been 20°50 of Pisces; and therefore, from such a determination of the planets, I would have been most fortunate with magnates and friends, as I have already stated above.

Furthermore, besides the two systems above that were thought up by their authors, two others can be made that are more reasonable, dividing the *Caelum* by circles drawn through the intersection of the horizon and the meridian.

The first, dividing the two rising arcs of the ecliptic of Porphyry individually into three equal parts, through which are passed those circles. The second, dividing the two semidiurnal and semi-nocturnal Alchabitius arcs individually into three parts, through which

---

who added the notable treatise, *On the Conjunctions of the Planets*, never hitherto published, with John of Saxony's Commentary'. John Danko of Saxony was a learned astronomer of the 15th century. His *Commentary on Alchabitius* was written in 1431. See Lynn Thorndike, HMES 3, Chapter XVII.

[1]But it is plain that Ptolemy was speaking of the Equal House System of house division with the minor change of reckoning that the 5 degrees above the ASC degree belonged to the 1st house, and then putting the 11th house in sextile to those ecliptical degrees, the MC in square to them, and the 9th house in trine. It is inconceivable that Ptolemy, the premier astronomer of antiquity, would have devised some other scheme of House Division without explaining it.

are passed those same circles that designate the oblique ascensions of the rising house in the equator, the poles of which would have to be found. And these two systems, because they absolve the division of the *Caelum* or the mundane space by those intersections of the horizon and the meridian that Nature has indicated, come closer to Nature and to the truth than those that were hitherto rejected, but they are therefore also erroneous because they are of no use when the ecliptic does not intersect the horizon, as [happens] under the arctic circle and beyond it.

Moreover, the true and natural method of dividing the *Caelum* ought to be universal for the whole Earth; otherwise astrology will not be a universal science, but only a particular and local one, which is alien to the reason of science. Besides, it will be plain below, that neither the ecliptic nor the parallel of the rising degree of the ecliptic should be primarily divided; and if the four above said modes are committed to experience, as was already done above for the Equal House System, their falsity will be even more plain.

Chapter 4. *In which the Method of Campanus for the Division of the* Caelum *into Astrological Houses is Particularly Examined by Reason and by Experience; and it is Compared to the Rational Method; and which of These is Declared to be Legitimate.*

Not without reason should a special chapter be devoted to this Campanus[1] method; first, on account of the author's fame, by which many are attracted; and then because this method offers no mean kind of probability. For it also divides the *Caelum* led by Nature through sections of the horizon and the meridian, like the Rational mode, and in addition it always divides the whole *Caelum*

---

[1]Campanus of Novara (1233-1296) was probably the premier mathematician of his time. He devised the Campanus System of computing the intermediate house cusps, but he never made any tables of houses, and calculating the cusps required a knowledge of trigonometry that few astrologers of that time possessed, so his system never caught on. It was, however, revived for a time by Cyril Fagan in the 20th century.

into 12 equal portions,[1] when all the rest [of the systems] divide it into very unequal parts, especially in the oblique sphere.

And for these reasons it can be universal, like the Rational System, and in practice it does not very frequently differ from the truth, as do the others rejected above; indeed, it often agrees with the Rational in the fundamentals of judgments, since the width of the houses and the signs brings it about that in a figure erected at the same moment according to both systems, all the planets are found, either in the same houses or the rulers of the same houses,[2] which also happens in the two systems made by me [and mentioned] above.

And so it must definitely be stated here that both of the two systems, namely that of Campanus and the Rational must be chosen and held to be both legitimate and natural, especially since already most of the astrologers follow the Rational System itself [following] after Abraham Avenezra[3] [c.1089-1167] and John Regiomontanus [1436-1476]; and it must be seen in what way these two systems agree and in what way they differ.

Therefore, in this they agree: *First*, that both of them divide the *Caelum* and the whole space of the World into four equal parts. *Second*, that they absolve the division of the oriental part by circles of position passed through intersections of the horizon and the meridian. *Third*, that they find the altitude of the pole above the individual circles of position and their oblique ascension on the equa-

---

[1] The Campanus System divides the *Caelum* into 12 uniform sections like the segments of an orange.

[2] Actually, the Campanus cusps and the Regiomontanus cusps can differ by many degrees, especially in the higher latitudes. If in a particular chart the house positions of the planets remain the same, this is a coincidence in a particular case, and not a general rule. For instance in Morin's chart for Wallenstein, Mars is in the 8th house by the Regiomontanus division, but in the 7th house by the Campanus division.

[3] This is not true of Abraham Ibn Ezra. He apparently used the Alchabitius system, but in one of his tracts, *The Book of the Fundamentals of the Tables*, he actually explains the rudiments of the Placidus system. See my paper "House Division II" in the AFA *Journal of Research*, vol. 5, no. 2 (1989): 33-52.

tor. *Fourth*, that from the individual oblique ascensions for the altitude of the pole of each circle of position, they find a conformable arc of the ecliptic. *Fifth*, that both systems divide the circle that is primary, and that they can divide the houses everywhere, with exception only for points on Earth exactly placed under the poles of the World, where every scheme of division by the circles mentioned fails.[1]

But in this they differ: First, because the mode of Campanus divides the rising part primarily by the vertical circle that is described through the rising and setting equinoctial into 6 equal parts, having taken its beginning from the zenith itself; and secondarily, it divides the equator, and from it the ecliptic. But the Rational System primarily divides the rising part also into 6 equal parts, having taken its beginning from the meridian circle, and secondarily [it divides] the ecliptic. Finally, the Campanus System always divides the *Caelum* into 12 equal parts, and then the equator and the ecliptic, except when the poles of these circles are found in the intersection of the horizon and the meridian, which happens for the pole of the equator in the right sphere, and for the pole of the ecliptic in the place with latitude 23°30 . And in the more oblique sphere, this system divides both the equator and the ecliptic into greatly unequal parts; indeed, many times it does not intersect the ecliptic above or below the Earth.

But the Rational System always cuts the equator into equal parts, just as it does the whole *Caelum* only in the right sphere; but it constantly cuts the ecliptic into unequal parts when it happens that it can be cut, just as it also cuts the *Caelum* beyond the right sphere; and the inequality of the parts of both the ecliptic and the *Caelum* turns out to be more, in which the sphere was more oblique; indeed, under the arctic circle and beyond many times too it does not intersect the ecliptic, either above or below the Earth.

---

[1]The Regiomontanus and the Campanus systems, like all the other quadrant systems (including the Placidus system), fail in the polar regions. Only the Morinus system, the Equal House system, and the original Sign-House system divide the sky without any difficulty there.

Having explained these things, since it is generally admitted by all that the astrological houses must be established by the division of some circle, it now follows that it must be seen which circle should be divided. Moreover, it is worthy of note that there is a three-fold difference in the sphere of the circles, that is of the terrestrial, celestial, and mixed. The terrestrial circle is unique, namely the horizon, which is the greatest circle on Earth, from which the place of the Native is described as the pole, through which for a man located in that pole, the *Caelum* is divided into two parts as judged by the senses, of which one is seen above the Earth, and the other lurks below the Earth; and so this circle is conceived to be extended from the circle to the *Caelum*; the horizon is not made a proper part of the *Caelum*, but only by transfer, dividing the *Caelum* itself into two parts, and the whole mundane space.

The celestial circle is the one that is so much more related to the *Caelum*, and it does not depend upon the Earth, such as the equator, the ecliptic, the colures, and then the circles of latitude and declination, for all of these would also be in the *Caelum* without the Earth. But the mixed circle is that which is indeed described in the *Caelum* but is dependent upon the Earth or the horizontal circle, that is related to a [particular] place on Earth, and these are all the vertical circles that pass from the pole of the horizon and are transferred to the *Caelum*, which is the meridian [circle] passing through the poles of the horizon and the World, then the circles of position passed through the sections of the horizon and the meridian. And these three kinds of circles happen in the division of the space of the *Caelum* or the World for the astrological houses, as will be plain below. Truly, that the vertical [circle] passing through the equinoctial rising and setting must not be divided primarily, as Campanus would have it, because it is neither celestial nor universal, but particular, nor does it have any virtue of its own as the meridian, the horizon, and other circles of position have. Second, because it is only assumed that the *Caelum* must be divided into equal parts, but although for the equal division of it by sections of the horizon and the meridian the *Caelum* might be cut into equal parts, and it might seem that this division is therefore founded on Nature, because both the horizon alone and the meridian, along with the horizon, are already dividing the *Caelum* into equal portions.

Nevertheless, Campanus erred in this, because he did not realize that the *Caelum* must not be divided into astrological houses by reason of its material or substance, but by reason of the motion by which it rises above the horizon and descends below it, it affects and changes the Native and the rest of the sublunar things. For if the *Caelum* would stand still, first that ought to be divided or indeed would be moved, but it would always affect the Native in the same manner, as happens under the pole of the World, with the *Caelum* itself uniformly revolving around the Native placed in the center of the horizon, without the ascent of any part or its descent above and below the horizon; then, no division of the houses would be possible, because there would be no rising, culminating, or setting,[1] and yet the *Caelum* from the terrestrial circle or the horizon would be divided into two equal parts, again divisible into two or six other equal parts, but not determined by those points which are not present under the poles due to the lack of a meridian.

Therefore, the division of the *Caelum* must not be made by reason of its substance, but by reason of its motion, since as a gift of the prime motion, it is to make the signs and the planets to go around through the individual houses, and in them to disperse the influxes of the stars; thus the gift of the division of the *Caelum* into those houses is to produce that motion at a given moment of time and to exhibit the state of the *Caelum* as a quiescent thing in a natal figure; and consequently that division of the *Caelum* by the vertical circle that Campanus thought up is merely fictitious. Truly if experience is joined to reasons, its falsity will be even more evident.

---

[1] But, as explained in a previous note, at the North Pole the ASC is 0 Libra and the DSC is 0 Aries. By either the Equal House system or the Sign-house System, there are 12 houses.

76

The Figure of my Nativity According to Campanus.

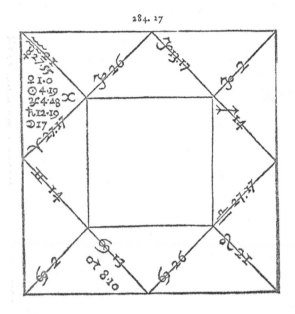

For in my nativity, shown here according to the Campanus System, the 9th cusp will be at 2 Capricorn, and so Saturn will be the ruler of the 9th for me; but from my tenderest years a perpetual zeal for the Catholic Religion supported me, in the bosom of which by the grace of God I was born and baptized, and which in France, Germany, Hungary, and elsewhere among Hussites, Lutherans, and Calvinists I boldly confessed, without ever any vacillation or doubt.

And this natural and fixed inclination in my religion is one of the notable things in my life that could not be gotten from the mobile sign Capricorn or its ruler Saturn,[1] even though it is here conjoined to Jupiter. For Jupiter would be dejected on the cusp of the 9th, like Saturn in the ASC, from which such an inclination could

---

[1]But many astrologers would consider that Capricorn and Saturn were appropriate significators of a religion that is old, rigid, and authoritarian.

not arise. But if the figure as above should be erected according to the Rational System, then Jupiter will be the ruler of the 9th, which is the [House] of Religion, powerful by triplicity in the ASC as the primary significator of inclinations, conjoined to the Sun, which in the 9th [would be] in its triplicity, and powerful in the ASC by triplicity and exaltation, applying by trine to Mars, ruler of the ASC and of the triplicity of the 9th, and also receiving all the planets, with the exception of Mercury, in their own dignities, and the cusps of the 1st and the 9th are in partile trine; therefore, viewed by nature, by state, by rulership and configuration, Jupiter and the cusp in trine aspect, it will be agreeable to any astrologer from the precepts that will be set forth below that these are the genuine causes of that inclination. To these add that in the Campanus System I would not have had the Heart of Scorpio in the 8th house, which very often cast me into the danger of violent death.

Again, in the nativity of Walstein, the duke of Friedland, the cusp of the 8th according to Campanus would be the 14th degree of Scorpio, and so Mars would be in the 7th, and if anyone would have said that a violent death would always have been signified by the direction of the MC to the square of Mars, although Mars was in the 7th, nevertheless because the 7th is the House of Open Enemies, death would rather be signified by the principles of astrology from a duel, or from a battle [waged] by open enemies. But he was traitorously slain by secret enemies, on account of Mars, which is found exalted in the 12th with Venus in the 8th, receiving themselves mutually by domicile.

Besides, Mars is found in both systems to be ruler of the 1st,[1] and consequently the significator of life, and therefore in the Campanus System it would not have been such a pernicious anaereta; but in the Rational System it is entirely lethal, because the ruler of the 1st in the 8th, especially when it is malefic by nature, portends a violent death; and so in this nativity it is more con-

---

[1] Again we note that the ASC sign is Aquarius, with all of Pisces intercepted and 26 degrees of Aries. Whence, the choice of Mars as ruler of the 1st seems rather arbitrary.

formably put in the 8th according to the Rational System than in the 7th according to Campanus.

Besides, here is displayed the nativity of François de Bonne [1543-1626], who from being a simple noble was made the Duke of Lesdiguières and Marshal of France, and finally Constable [of France] by the very famous man, Jacques Valois, formerly his domestic, now the General Treasurer of France in Dauphiné, very learned in astronomy and astrology. His chart was erected according to the Rational System, based on which I predicted the time of the death of that man,[1] when I was consulted about that same matter by Lord Valois himself, and in which [chart] Mars, ruler of the 11th and the Sun is in the 11th with Mercury, ruler of the ASC, received by domicile in turn by Venus; and that brought him the friendship of soldiers, knights, and captains, and most fortunate success from them. But according to the Campanus System the cusp of the 12th would have been 8 Taurus, and so Mars would have been in the 12th, and Saturn in opposition to it from the 6th, mutually applying; consequently, signifying imprisonments, illnesses, and great evils, from which that Native was perpetually free; therefore, the system of Campanus does not agree with experience.

But not even the horizon, the terrestrial circle, or the meridian or the mixed circle should be divided, since on the contrary these and the rest of the circles of position are dividing, also in the Campanus System; therefore, it remains that the circle that ought to be divided is solely the celestial circle. Consequently, since the circles of latitude, declination, and the colures are also dividing the equator and the ecliptic, of which the former is the prime circle, but they represent these according to motion; therefore, one or the other of these will have to be divided primarily; but not the ecliptic, on account of the reasons that have very often been said. Therefore, the equator alone necessarily remains to be divided primarily, and no reason why this should be rejected can be given,

---

[1] That is, the death of Constable Lesdiguières.

The Nativity of François de Bonne, Constable of France.

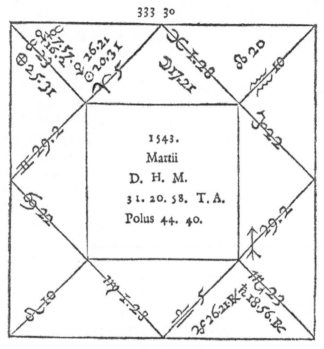

[Saint-Bonnet-en-Champsaur] 44°40′ N
1 April 1543 8:58 A.M.

since there is no possible division of the houses unless it is divided, as was already stated above. But the mystery of this division must be repeated profoundly and disclosed more clearly.

To erect a figure or to divide the *Caelum* with respect to the Earth, Nature displays two circles—the equator, which is celestial, and the horizon, which is terrestrial, dividing themselves into two parts, for where they coincide there is no division of the houses. Furthermore, because the *Caelum* ought to be divided at the point on the Earth for which the figure is going to be erected, and not the Earth at any point on the *Caelum*; therefore, not the horizon, but the equator itself must be divided; not, however, by points of the intersections of both of the circles, for having passed the circles through them, neither of these are subdivided, not even through the poles of the horizon or the equator, for thus the horizon would also be divided, which should not be divided; therefore, the subdivision of the equator must be continued through those very poles of the equator and the horizon that Nature indicates.

For not in vain does she supply those points to us, and it is beyond reason that any others might be fabricated; but now the circle that is drawn through those poles, and the meridian, which along with the horizon cuts the equator, or the circle of prime motion, into four equal parts, of which the points of the section are called cardinal points; and of these, one is at the rising, another at the MC, another at the setting, and the last at the IMC, differing among themselves in virtue. And each of these has two others of the same nature in the equator itself—those namely with which it makes an equilateral triangle, from which it results that this actual quaternary division does by virtue contain twelve points, not being continued through other points, but rather through those in which the two prime circles dividing the equator, that is the horizon and the meridian, are now intersecting each other; whence, this division must by the best judgment be said to be Rational, because it follows Nature and reason in all things, and it distributes the very motion of the *Caelum* equally through the several houses, so that each point of the equator stays as long in one house as it does in another, however the *Caelum* itself is unequally divided; indeed, it emulates the Divine Trinity, on account of the trine—that number of the circles, which are the complete foundation of the above said division.

Furthermore, of the circles dividing the equator into the astrological houses, the primary one is the horizon itself, both because the horizon is given without the meridian, as under the pole, but there is no meridian without a horizon, because it must necessarily be traced through the pole [of the horizon], and because the horizon alone determines the celestial figure. If in fact a unique meridian coincides with the same horizon, many horizons can also coincide with the same meridian, with only the latitude of the place being changed.

But the circle that is second in dignity among those doing the dividing is the meridian circle itself, both because without a meridian no division of the *Caelum* into houses is possible,[1] and no other circles of position are given that depend upon [both] the horizon and the meridian, and then because it succeeds the horizon in order, for it first cuts the *Caelum* into two equal parts, but the meridian separates both of those into two other [parts that are] also equal, and a minor subdivision is made from the other circles of position.

And so, the horizon and the meridian are the two primary circles of the whole natal figure, which therefore Nature has ennobled before the rest with the privilege of outstanding virtue, and this was also observed and marveled at by JoFrancus Offusius,[2] the hater of astrology, who was otherwise a learned and precise man, from whom Kepler selected many things, and yet he confessed that he did not know their cause.

Finally, since of the celestial circles only the equator is suitable for dividing the *Caelum* for the differentiation of the astrological houses, it cannot be denied that it agrees with the universal virtue with respect to the houses, which is determined by the actual division of the equator itself, which must be noted incidentally for what follows. Add to this that when Ptolemy in *Quadripartite*, Book 3, Chapter 10, will have the 11th house to aspect the ASC by sextile, the 10th to aspect it by square, and the 9th to aspect it by

---

[1]Not strictly true! The Equal House method of house division depends solely upon the ASC degree, which is at the intersection of the ecliptic and the horizon. The meridian plays no part in that system.

[2]A reference to his book, *De divina astrorum facultate facultate in larvatam astrologiam* (Paris, 1570) 'On the Divine Power of the Stars Against a Bewitched Astrology'. See Thorndike, HMES 6, pp. 22-24, 108-111. Offusius (c.1500-c.1565) was a medical doctor who had denounced traditional astrology and devised a new system. Consequently, he denounced other astrologers who were using traditional systems. Morin therefore classified him as an opponent of astrology.

trine, these aspects can only be understood to be in the equator, and also he means for the division of the houses to pertain primarily to the equator.[1] See our notes on the *Commentary on the Centiloquium*, Aphorism 37, published by Lord de Villennes.[2]

Chapter 5. *In which the Rational System of Dividing is Set Forth as the More Accurate Method; and a Notable Difficulty About that System is Resolved, Along with a New Division of the Houses by that Same Rational System.*

There are two ways in which the *Caelum* is divided into the astrological houses according to the Rational System; namely, by Tables of Houses and by Tables of Ascensions. But because the Tables of Houses are not drawn out for individual degrees of the altitude of the pole, as are the Tables of Ascensions; therefore, we shall only explain the latter way here, as being the more accurate way.

And so, let the figure of my nativity be erected for the year 1583, on the day of 22 February, at 20:33 hours of Apparent Time, at Villefranche, Beaujolais, by the Rudolphine Tables. The difference of the meridians is 0:28, to which must also be added the Equation of Time 0:15. Similarly, these must be added, according to the seventh part of the Science of Longitudes; and consequently the equated and corrected time is 21:16, for which the true places of the individual planets are collected from those tables. Moreover, the true place of the Sun is 4°19′ 18″, of which the Right Ascension is 336°12′. But given the Apparent Time of 20:33, converted into degrees of the equator it is 308°15′, which with the

---

[1]This was Regiomontanus's belief, which Morin adopted. But it is wrong.! Ptolemy was referring to the Equal House system and consequently to the division of the ecliptic, not the equator.

[2]Nicolas de Bourdin, Marquess of Villennes (d. 1670), *Le Centilogve de Ptolomee* (Paris: Cardin Besongne, 1651). It is cited and commented upon by Morin in his *Remarques Astrologiques* (Paris: Pierre Menard, 1657), of which there is a fine modern edition with an Introduction and notes by Jacques Halbronn, *Remarques Astrologiques sur le Commentaire du Centiloque de Ptolomée par Nicolas Bourdin* (Paris: Retz, 1976).

Right Ascension of the Sun makes 284°27' for the Right Ascension of the MC, for which in the Table of Right Ascensions is equivalent to 13°17' Capricorn. Moreover, if 30° is added to the right Ascension, and to that sum another 30°, and that is repeated 5 times, there will arise 314°27', 344°27', 14°27', [44°27'], and 74°27' for the Oblique Ascensions of the oriental houses 11, 12, 1, 2, and 3, that must be divided by the circles of position drawn through the sections of the horizon and the meridian, above which must be individually found the altitude of the pole, given by the Rational Table of Houses according to Regiomontanus[1]; and it is put here for the sake of greater convenience and readier explanation.

In the column of the Latitude of the Place (*Latitudo loci*), the latitude of the place of my nativity or of the horizon is sought, which is 45°25'; if this would have been only 45°, there would be had in the two columns to the right 26°34' for the altitude of the pole above the circles of position of the 11th and the 3rd houses, as well as 40°54' for the altitude of the pole of the circles [of position] of the 12th and the 2nd [houses]. But because the latitude of the place of my nativity is 45°25', it will therefore be necessary [to make] a double entry into the Table and to find a proportional part, as is customarily done in tables, and 26°54' will be found[2] for the exact altitude of the pole above the circles of position of the 11th and the 3rd houses, as well as 41°19' for the altitude of the pole of the 12th and the 2nd.

Therefore, in the Tables of Oblique Ascension for those latitudes, or the altitudes of the pole, the Oblique Ascensions given above are sought, and on the right the degree of the ecliptic corresponding to those same ascensions, having made a double entry into the Tables, and 1°38' Aquarius is found for the 11th house,

---

[1]*Tabulae directionum profectionumque...in nativitatibus multum utiles* (Augsburg: Erhard Ratdolt, 1490. often reprinted) 'Tables of Directions and Profections...Very Useful in Nativities'.

[2]The Latin text has 26°45' by mistake for 26°54', evidently a typographical error. I have corrected it in the translation.

Rational Table of Houses

Latitudo Loci Gr.	Domus 11. 3 G. M.	Domus 12. 2 G. M.	Latitudo Loci Gr.	Domus 11. 3. G. M.	Domus 12. 2. G. M.
1	0. 29	0. 51	31	16. 44	27. 49
2	0. 59	1. 43	32	17. 21	28. 25
3	1. 29	2. 25	33	17. 59	29. 11
4	1. 59	3. 27	34	18. 38	30. 17
5	2. 29	4. 19	35	19. 18	31. 14
6	3. 0	5. 11	36	19. 58	32. 11
7	3. 31	6. 4	37	20. 39	33. 8
8	4. 2	6. 57	38	21. 20	34. 5
9	4. 32	7. 49	39	22. 2.	35. 2
10	5. 3	8. 41	40	22. 45	36. 0
11	5. 34	9. 33	41	23. 29.	36. 58
12	6. 5.	10. 26	42	24. 14	37. 57
13	6. 36	11. 18	43	25. 0	38. 56
14	7. 7	12. 11	44	25. 47	39. 55
15	7. 38	13. 4	45	26. 34	40. 54
16	8. 9	13. 57	46	27. 22	41. 53
17	8. 41	14. 50	47	28. 11.	42. 53
18	9. 13	15. 43	48	29. 2	43. 53
19	9. 45	16. 36	49	29. 54	44. 54
20	10. 18	17. 30	50	30. 57	45. 55
21	10. 51	18. 23	51	31. 41	46. 56
22	11. 25	19. 17	52	32. 37	47. 57
23	11. 58	20. 11	53	33. 34	48. 59
24	12. 32	21. 5	54	34. 32	50. 1.
25	13. 7	21. 59	55	35. 32	51. 3
26	13. 42	22. 53	56	36. 33	52. 5.
27	14. 18	23. 48	57	37. 35	53. 8
28	14. 54	24. 43	58	38. 39	54. 11
29	15. 30	25. 38	59	39. 45	55. 14
30	16. 7	26. 33	60	40. 53	56. 13

[This is what would now be called a Table of the Regiomontanus Poles of the Houses]

3°18′ Pisces for the 12th, 27°17′ for the ASC, 6°32′ Gemini for the 2nd, and 27°14′ Gemini for the 3rd house, with the opposite of these houses in the occidental part of the *Caelum*, [viz.] 4, 5, 6, 7, 8, and 9, corresponding to the opposite degrees of the ecliptic.

And this is the way of constructing the figure accurately by Tables—the best and easiest of all, and the only one agreeing with Ptolemy's opinion on the aspect of houses 11, 10, and 9 to the ASC, namely with the aspects taken in the equator,[1] by which it is also easy to discern in what house any planet is by center or body. As in my nativity the altitude of the pole above the circle of position of the 11th house is 41°19′, but above the circles of position of Mercury, Venus, and the Sun it is 40°30′, 40°56′, and 41°18′.

Therefore, these planets, with the exception of the Sun, are not centrally [located] in the 12th but rather above it. The circle of position of Jupiter and the Moon is 41°24′ and 41°25′. Therefore, these two planets are in the same circle of position, and in almost the same one as the circle [of position] of the 12th house, but within it; and so with the others. Furthermore, the planets are put in the figure according to the series of their own Right Ascensions, for the Right Ascensions of those that go before precede in the diurnal motion.

Truly, although Nature supplied only this Rational System to us, yet a huge difficulty with it remains to be unraveled.[2] For even though the equator is divisible by circles of position on the whole globe of Earth, the ecliptic however is not everywhere divided by them. But from the polar circles to the poles of the World it often coincides with the horizon or with another circle of position; that is, in latitude 66°30′ it coincides with the horizon on all individual days; in latitude 69°22′ it coincides with the circle of position of the 12th house, and in latitude 77°44′ it coincides with the circle

---

[1] Again it should be mentioned that Ptolemy intended the aspects that he mentions to be reckoned in the ecliptic, not in the equator as Regiomontanus supposed.

[2] Here, Morin begins to explain the Universal Rational system as he calls it, but which is nowadays called the Morinus system.

of the 11th; and then it seems that it cannot be defined as to the rulership of which planet a house is under beginning from that circle, but it seems that it is under the rulership of no planet at all, because those circles neither intersect the ecliptic, nor do they coincide with it.

This, moreover, will be intolerable in astrology—that is, every house or its signification ought to be subject to the rulership of some planet. And in short they are indeed given the oblique ascensions of those houses and their circles of position, but there are no degrees of the ecliptic corresponding to them. And so, from the polar circles to the poles of the World, the Rational System is seen not to be universal, but only local—consequently not scientific, but vain or erroneous. [1]

Nevertheless, it must *first* be noted that the twelfths or the signs of the zodiac are divided by circles of latitude passed through the poles of the ecliptic, and therefore they are extended from one pole to the other, individually comprising the twelve parts of the whole *Caelum*. *Second*, that the Moon, for example, the ruler of Cancer, rules that whole sign, according as it extends from one pole of the ecliptic to the other, and not just those arcs of the ecliptic that intersect the ecliptic itself at its middle; and therefore, a planet that is in Cancer beyond the ecliptic is nevertheless said to be under the dominion of the Moon, and she is its ruler.

And the same thing must be judged about any other sign and its ruler. *Third*, that in the middle of the twelfths, through which the ecliptic passes, the greatest efficacy of virtue exists in those signs; whence it results that the greatest relationship is always had from the ecliptic, just as if the whole force of the signs reposed only in the ecliptic; and that is evidently proved by directions, from which is established not only that the direction of a significator to a planet

---

[1] This same objection applies to all the quadrant systems except the Porphyry system and the Alchabitius system. Those simply trisect the arcs between the MC and the ASC, but the Campanus, Regiomontanus, Placidus, and Koch systems that use more elaborate calculations to establish the cusps of the intermediate houses all fail in the polar regions.

seen with its latitude is effective, but also seen at its place in the ecliptic.[1]

Indeed the Head and Tail of the Dragon, [considered to be] of such great virtue among the ancients, have no other force than that they are points on the ecliptic, in which the Moon is thought to be strongest in her own nodes.

Having settled these matters, since the equator is divided by circles of position into points that are the beginnings of the houses, the longitudes of these points on the equator may be found, or the degrees of the zodiac to which they belong; and so, the sign of each house and consequently the planet of that sign, that is the rulers of that sign are known. So, moreover, their longitudes will be found.

There are had, as above, the ascensions of the six oriental houses; and because from the ascension of each house the intercepted arc of the equator is given, between the beginnings of Aries and Libra, and the point of ascension of each house, with the ecliptic, and with the circle of latitude delimiting that ascension; and from that, there is made a right triangle at the intersection of the ecliptic with the circle of latitude, in which is always known the above said arc and the angle between it and the ecliptic, which is the maximum Obliquity of the Ecliptic, or 23°30'. Therefore, let there always be made the tangent of the complement of that arc times the sine of the complement of the Obliquity of the Ecliptic as the radius to the tangent of the elliptical arc, which will indicate the sign and the degree of the beginning of each house.

But note in particular that if the ascension is less than the quadrant of a circle, it must be worked with that, and it will produce an arc of the ecliptic counted from the beginning of Aries.

If the ascension is greater than a quadrant and less than a semicircle, it must be worked with the complement of that ascension to

---

[1]Here Morin asserts what he also says elsewhere that a valid direction may be made to both the mundane position of a planet and to its zodiacal position.

the semicircle, and it will produce the semi-ecliptical complement counted from Aries to Libra.

If the ascension surpasses a semicircle, and is yet less than three quarters of a circle, or 270°, it must be worked with its excess over the semicircle, and it will produce an arc of the ecliptic counted from the beginning of Libra. And finally, if the ascension surpasses ¾ of a circle, it will have to be worked with the complement to the whole circle, and it will produce a semi-ecliptical complement counted from Libra to Aries. And having done this always and everywhere, the cusps of the houses will be had by sign and degree; and it will also be known to which planet they are subject.[1]

Therefore, having reduced these [rules] to practice in my nativity, of which the [oblique] ascensions of the oriental houses are given above, by calculation there will be produced the following beginnings of those houses, namely those that are discerned in the following figure. Since the points of the *Caelum* in which the equator and the circles of position intersect correspond to those degrees of the zodiac, these are their longitudes.

---

[1]These rather involved rules may be more simply restated as follows. Add multiples of 30° to the RAMC to get the Oblique Ascension of houses 11, 12, 1, 2, and 3. Multiply the tangent of the RAMC and that of each of these derived OA's by the cosine of the Obliquity of the Ecliptic. Then find the arc tangent of the products. If the RAMC or the OA is between 0° and 90°, the arc tangent is the longitude of the cusp. If the RAMC or the OA is between 90° and 270°, the arc tangent + 180° is the longitude of the cusp. If the RAMC or the OA is between 270° and 360°, the arc tangent + 360° is the longitude of the cusp.

The Figure of My Nativity Erected According to the Rational & Universal System.

284. 27

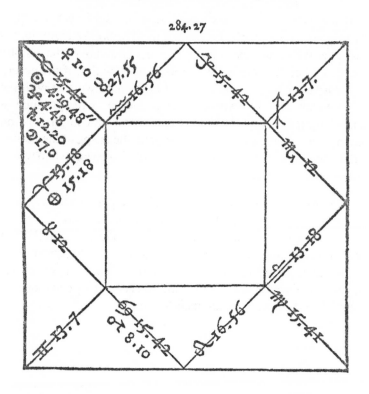

And having accepted this, the Rational system is rendered Universal for the whole Earth, concerning which two things are worthy of note. First, that no sign is ever intercepted in the houses of the figure. Second, that all the figures erected at the same instant of time under the same meridian have these same house cusps in the ecliptic, whatever may be the altitude of the pole above the horizon, or the diversity of the horizon, namely because they have the same ascensions of the houses, and in fact for any point on the equator there is the same and unique longitude in the ecliptic; but the points differ in this—that on the right sphere the parts of the *Caelum* divided into houses agree more closely with equality; but the more oblique the sphere is, the more the parts of the *Caelum* are unequal among themselves.[1]

But since the virtue of each sign thrives at its most in the ecliptic, as was already said above, therefore where it happens that the circles of the houses are cut simultaneously by the equator and the ecliptic, the degree of the ecliptic itself will have to be especially observed for the determination of the principal ruler of the cusp; if the rulership happens to be divided, that is if the point of the same circle of position is cut by the equator and the ecliptic, they will belong to signs of different planets; therefore, the degree of the ecliptic corresponding in longitude to the section of the equator, will then be only a secondary or Prior Vicar for that rulership; but no particular observation is made of the rest of the points of the *Caelum* placed between the equator and the ecliptic on the same horizon or on another circle of position, although they are also subject to the rulership of the planets and are reduced in longitude to the ecliptic; that is, because the division of the houses should only be made by something determined, which are the points of the intersection of the equator or the ecliptic by a circle of position, but not by those intermediate points.

However, it is useful to observe the transits of the planets, not only over that point of the ecliptic intersected by the horizon or by another circle of position, either in the degree of that same ecliptic corresponding to the intersected degree of the equator, but also in the intermediate degrees, which, when a planet traverses it, there easily arises an effect according to the signification of the house to which that circle of position belongs—especially when it is actually on that circle of position, but less when beyond it, although it is in the same house; for beyond it, it does not belong to its signifi-

[1]But a third thing should be noted. The longitude of the MC will be slightly different from the true longitude; and the longitude of the ASC will be considerably different from the true longitude. The Alexandrians, who invented horoscopic astrology, emphasized that the ASC degree was the most important point in the *Caelum* and the basis of the other houses of the horoscope. Consequently, the Morinus system of houses fails to conform to that fundamental principle of house division.

cation from its own location. Besides, since planets project their own rays on the circle, it will be useful to take note of their aspects to the points of the equator intersected by the circles of position, for these aspects are effective.

Finally, since the Part of Fortune can also not be extracted anywhere on Earth without all the methods of the ancients, so it may be elicited universally by this method. The ascension of the Sun is subtracted from the ascension of the Moon, taken always in the proper circle of position of that light, and the remainder is added to the ascension of the ASC; an arc of the equator results, the longitude of which will have to be found as above, and the Part of Fortune must be located in the degree found. For thus the distance of the Part of Fortune is as much from the Moon as is the distance of the Sun from the ASC in degrees of the equator.[1]

Either measure the degrees of the equator intercepted between the circles of position of the Sun and the ASC and add them to the Right Ascension of the Moon if it is in the meridian, [or to] the oblique [ascension] if it is beyond it, and the same degree of the equator is produced as above.

Furthermore, that the doctrine above is lacking neither in logic nor in experience must be proved by a few things. Moreover, the logic is this: if there is a universal force in the equator with respect to the astrological houses, as was shown at the end of Section II, Chapter 4, it is also certain that its consideration should not be neglected here. Indeed, Ptolemy at the end of *Tetrabiblos*, Book 3, Chapter 10, when he will have the ASC to be aspected by a sextile to the 11th, by a square to the 10th, and by a trine to the 9th, means only a division of the houses by means of the equator, as we have already said at the end of Section II, Chapter 4.[2]

---

[1] This instruction is somewhat similar to the method of Negusantius for finding the mundane position of the Part of Fortune. Namely, subtract the OA of the Sun from the RA of the Moon and add the difference to the OA of the ASC; the result is the RA of the Part of Fortune, whose declination is the same as the Moon's.
[2] But see the note to that chapter.

But the individual degrees of it are referred in longitude to degrees of the ecliptic; and therefore, two degrees of both circles corresponding to each other belong to the same planet by rulership; therefore, from the given sixth point of the equator, there is given a planet to be the ruler in that section that must by no means be disparaged as the Vicar, indeed laying claim to pre-eminence for itself as ruler, either when the equator alone is cut by the circle of position or when the ecliptic coincides with some circle of position.

And this squares nicely with itself, for when the ecliptic coincides with the horizon, it cannot be said that any planet rules the first house or the ASC, but neither is it true that Saturn, Jupiter, Mars, Venus, and Mercury are ruling the signs from Capricorn to Cancer, which comprise the oriental hemicycle, or truly ruling the ASC itself, since in that hemicycle there is given a point for the true ASC, either more effective for the Native in the rising—that is, that which is in the rising of the equinoctial World according to the Cabala of the Houses.

But in that point, the equator intersects the horizon; that is the ecliptic at the beginning of Aries, which point Mars rules; therefore, Mars may be said to be at least the primary ruler of the ASC above the rest of the planets that also rule that same oriental hemicycle. If anyone shall have said, who, therefore will be the primary ruler of the 12th, the 11th, the 10th, etc., since the whole ecliptic is on the horizon? The answer is that he will be the unique ruler who rules the point on the equator that is cut by the circle of position of the 12th house, the 11th, the 10th etc., and so every difficulty is removed.

Finally too, in those individual systems of erecting the figure that were rejected above, the same inconvenience occurs from the whole ecliptic's being on the horizon, or on another circle of position, preventing the division of the *Caelum* and the rulerships of the planets over the individual houses, unless some circle other than the ecliptic is divided. And as above the planets rule the division by the points reduced to the ecliptic; therefore, the Rational System as set forth by us, must be preferred in all ways to the rest of them.

But as for that which pertains to experience, we are of course left in the lurch here for examples of men of the north in whose nativities the ecliptic is some circle of position. But in my nativity erected according to the doctrine [set forth] above, the cusps of the houses retain the same signs as in the ordinary Rational System, with the exception of the 2nd and the 8th, which here are Gemini and Sagittarius, but there are Taurus and Scorpio; nevertheless, both figures correspond outstandingly to my accidents, for in the ordinary system Mercury is the ruler of the 2nd house for me in nearly partile sextile with the ASC, and in the truth of the matter by my own talent and knowledge, [bestowed] however by the provident God, I have gained thus far from wherever I have lived but poorly, because Mercury has stimulated me more keenly to the sciences than to acquiring riches.

But in this newest system, Venus is the ruler of the 2nd for me, and in the truth of the matter, when the MC came by direction to Venus, the most illustrious Lord Marshall Dessiat, the Supreme Head of the Royal Treasury, gave to me without my request, nor indeed from himself, [but] well deservedly, more than 800 gold pieces, from just a most generous inclination towards men who were supporters of true sciences, and by me at least due praises here should be celebrated. Therefore, not in vain may Venus be said by me to be the secondary ruler of the 2nd house, and Mercury the primary ruler.

Similarly, in the ordinary system the fire sign Sagittarius with the violent fixed star Cor Scorpii[1] begins the 8th house for me, and Jupiter is ruler of the 8th in the 12th in Pisces and in the heart of the Sun,[2] and from such a cusp the dangers of a violent death were be-

---

1Antares or α Scorpii, which was in 3°57′ Sagittarius.
2That is, combust.

94

ing signified, but they were also being signified in the newest system by Scorpio's being found on the cusp of the 8th, namely because Mars is at the same time the ruler of the ASC and the 8th and [posited] in its own fall, with its ruler the Moon conjoined to Saturn in the 12th house.

And so, by fire, iron, waters, and horses I have fallen into amazing dangers of violent death, so that I now marvel and render thanks to the Divine Goodness, which alone preserved me from them, even when seriously and dangerously injured, with the agreement of the trine of Jupiter and of the whole cluster of planets to Mars from signs of little violence. Therefore, both the degree of the ecliptic and the degree of the equator cut by the circle of position are strong in virtue, and this will be verified here and there in other nativities, all of whose accidents are known.

Moreover, this doctrine can be confirmed otherwise by directions, of which nothing in astrology is more evident than their effects. But the directions must only be undertaken with the equator and not with the ecliptic; indeed, when the arc of direction is converted into time, it must be divided by the mean diurnal motion of the Sun in right ascension, which has to do with the equator and not with the ecliptic, as will be more fully explained by us elsewhere; therefore, it is completely proven that the force of the equator is the greatest force in astrology.

But some things occur that must be noted here with regard to the placement of the planets and fixed stars in the spaces of the figure, or in the astrological houses, of which some suit any sphere, but others only the oblique sphere.

And so in general, stars or points on the *Caelum*, whose northern declination is greater than the complement of the latitude of the place, never set, but are always located above the Earth, and consequently in the houses above the horizon, 12, 11, 10, 9, 8, or 7. But those whose southern declination is greater than the complement of the latitude of the place, never rise, but are always located beneath the horizon, and consequently in the houses below the Earth, 1, 2, 3, 4, 5, or 6. Moreover, from the tables of oblique ascensions, it is plain from their kind which points of the ecliptic are always above or below the horizon beyond latitude 66°30 . But the rest of the points of the Caelum rise and set.

With regard to this, in the northern sphere the stars and the points of the *Caelum* that are above the Earth are always rotating, but those whose declination is greater discharge their own rotation within the 9th and 10th houses above the Earth; and those whose declination is less extend their rotation to the 11th and the 8th; and they are found on the meridian twice in twenty-four hours, higher on the northern part and lower on the southern part. But then they are always in the 10th house; however, not on the southern part in the 10th and on the northern part in the 4th. For the whole semicircle of the meridian above the Earth pertains to the 10th house from what was said before; and therefore, from no point of the ecliptic that is south above the Earth and in the southern part; but anything that is of the northern part (namely, that which does not set) is said to be on the 10th cusp and its ruling planet will be the primary ruler of the 10th; moreover, the secondary ruler of the 10th will be the planet that is ruler of the opposite point that is underneath the Earth, which will correspond by right ascension with the point above the Earth occupying the meridian circle. But in turn, the secondary ruler of the 10th will be the primary ruler of the 4th; and the primary ruler of the 10th will be the secondary ruler of the 4th.

Whence, it is no wonder that experience proves that the things signified by these opposite houses are reciprocated, and [that it is possible] from the 10th to judge about the 4th, and in turn from the 4th to judge about the 10th; which understood, no perturbation of mind will arise that from the part of the north and not the part of the south we may seek the primary ruler of the 10th; since the ecliptic, by its own law and by the law of the meridian below the Earth, on that account calls forth our mind on account of its location in the northern places, very dissimilar, from which dissimilar effects are also produced.

And the same logic applies to all the other semicircles of the rest of the houses intercepted between the two sections of the horizon and the meridian towards both the northern and southern extremes of the World, which strengthens our previous judgment. For if the semicircles of the 9th and the 11th houses cut by the ecliptic near to the northern section of the horizon and the ecliptic are said to be under the rulerships of the planets which rule the sectional points of the ecliptic without any controversy among astrologers, no valid reason can be offered why the same things cannot be said for the intermediate semicircle of the meridian, which is cut by that same ecliptic.

Finally, it is certain that all the systems that divide the *Caelum* from the poles of the ecliptic or the equator that are found beyond the common section of the horizon and the meridian are false and contrary to experience, and only the Rational System is true, which always squares with experience. And so a star that is found in any point of the meridian above the Earth must be said to be in the 10th house, but in the 4th house if it is in the opposite semicircle.

Hence it is plain that Regiomontanus had not noticed this difficulty in Problem 17 of his Tables, when he asserts that if the right ascensions of any star and of the MC are different by 180 degrees, that star will be in the angle of the Earth, that is in the 4th house, since the right ascension of the MC always differs by 180 degrees from the right ascension of a star found on the meridian under the Earth, below the pole of the equator, when however that star is above the Earth.

Moreover, it must be carefully noted that the 10th house or its cusp or circle of position is one thing, and the MC is another thing. For the 10th or its circle of position is the entire semicircle of the meridian above the Earth, but the MC is the arc of that semicircle at which stars can ascend and then descend by their diurnal motion, namely being in the middle in the *Caelum* of their ascent and descent above the Earth; but this arc is only taken from the pole through the zenith to the southern horizon for the northern regions of the Earth. Therefore, whatever planet is direct to the MC is understood to be directed only to that arc, but not to the other remaining to it from the northern part (which two arcs the pole itself separates) or to a star placed in the remaining one, and so a planet can be on the cusp of the 10th when it is not in the MC.

Therefore, it seems that it only remains for us to teach by which method and order the planets and fixed stars are to be located in the spaces or the astrological houses. And so, **First**, take away from the right ascension of the star the right ascension of the MC, and if the remainder is null with northern declination, or even with a southern declination that is less than the complement of the latitude of the place, the planet is on the above said MC; but if the remainder is 180 degrees with a northern declination that is greater than the complement of the latitude of the place, the planet is in the 10th or the meridian above the Earth from the northern part. But if the north or south declination is less than what was just said, the planet will be in the 4th house or the meridian under the Earth. But if the remainder is less than 180 degrees, the planet is in the oriental or ascending half of the *Caelum*; and finally, if it is greater [than 180 degrees], the planet is in the occidental part.

Second. From what was said before, it will be established whether or not a planet or a fixed star can rise or set within twenty-four hours; and if not always nor more than twenty-four hours it remains above or below the horizon, then at the given latitude of the place, with the declination of the planet, its ascensional difference is taken from the Tables, and in the case of a northern declination it is added to 90 degrees, and in a southern declination it is subtracted from 90 degrees, and thus the semidiurnal arc of the star [is found].

And so, if a star is in the oriental half of the *Caelum* and its distance from the MC is less than that arc, the star will be above the Earth in the 12th, 11th, or 10th house. If it is greater, [it will be] below in the 1st, 2nd, or 3rd. Moreover, if the star is in the occidental half of the *Caelum*, and its distance from the MC is greater than that arc, it will be below the Earth in the 4th, 5th, or 6th; if it is less, [it will be] above in the 7th, 8th, or 9th house.

Finally, for whatever star or planet that is above or below the Earth it will be established from what was said before that the circle of position of the cusps of the figure may be found, and it will be plain in what space it must be placed; moreover, those stars posited in the same house should be placed in the same order as their right ascensions, as we have already said elsewhere. Or if [its distance from the MC] is greater, with their own circles and oblique ascensions; and so the celestial figure will be erected correctly at all locations. And from what was said previously, it is plain that the equator serves for the division of the houses, but the ecliptic for finding their rulers.

Incidentally however, it must be noted that all celestial figures that occur under the same parallel with the same numbered hour, during one revolution of the Primum Mobile, are very similar among themselves, if you make exception for the place of the Moon.[1] And therefore, those born on the same day under the same parallel and at the same numbered hour, are sufficiently subject to the same things. But those born at the same time under the same meridian in diverse latitudes, although they have all the planets in the same places in the zodiac, and the same MC, yet their figures are more dissimilar among themselves than the figures of those who are born at the same numbered hour under the same parallel,[2] as is plain for the construction of the figures.

See those things about the true method of erecting celestial figures that were stated by us in our French astrological notes against the Marquess of Villennes in his *Commentary* on Ptolemy's *Centiloquium*.[3]

---

[1]Morin refers to nativities erected at the same hour under the same latitude, but in different longitudes around the Earth. The house cusps would be very similar, but the Moon's longitude and that of the other planets would be different.

[2]And nativities erected at the same hour under different latitudes will have the planets in the same place, but the house cusps will be different.

[3]This refers to Morin's book, *Remarques astrologiques ... sur le Commentaire du*

SECTION III.

In which the Essence or the Formal Reason for the Astrological Houses is Stated.

Chapter 1. *The Essence of an Astrological House consists of the Relation of its Site to a Birth that takes place beyond the axis of the Pole.*

An astrological house is here taken by us only [as a term] for any of the parts of the astrological figure, by which in any place on Earth either the whole *Caelum* or the mundane space for the one being born is divided into twelve parts, which are called houses, diverse in virtue among themselves in accordance with the diverse site of each of them in it with respect to its division.

Furthermore, since the division of the houses is made by the relation of the site of each house to another, this will not be the center of the Earth, or any other point of the mundane axis, for the division of the houses cannot be made without a particular meridian, as was [made] plain in the preceding Section, but in the center and the whole axis of the World no particular meridian can be assigned; therefore, no distinction of houses is possible in the center or in the axis of the World. Therefore, [they cannot be made] under the poles,[1] which are the extremes of that axis.

Moreover, with a man placed beyond the center and the axis on the surface of the Earth, so that in that very place there is a particular meridian, and from that he is subjected to the appointed sites of the celestial bodies, and to the differences in their rising, culminating, and setting; so also of the division of the houses or of the sites it furnishes an origin for itself, as far as it is placed beyond the axis of the World.

Centiloque de Ptolémée mis en lumiere par Messire Nicolas de Bourdin, Chevalier, Marquis de Villennes ... (Paris: Pierre Menard, 1657), which was published posthumously. There is an excellent modern French edition with a valuable Introduction by Jacques Halbronn (Paris: Retz, 1976) 303 pp.

[1]That is, they cannot be made by the use of any of the quadrant systems of house division, as is mentioned in previous notes.

For a line drawn from the center of the World through [the place of] the Native, as it was established above, leaves off at the point of the *Caelum* that is called the Native's zenith or vertex, from which a horizontal circle is imagined to be drawn. And the circle that is passed through that zenith and through the poles of the equator separated by the horizon, that one is the meridian for the Native, but through the sections of these, the rest of the circles of position are extended as divisors of the houses.

From which, it is plain that the essence of an astrological house consists of the relation of its own simple site to the Native, or to the point on the surface of the Earth in which he is born, as far as it is located beyond the center and axis of the World; and so the astrological houses are essentially joined to that very point by reason of their site.

Chapter 2. *Whether the Division of the Houses is Made for the Center of the Earth, or Whether it is Made for the Place of Birth; and What is the Material Cause of These.*

Since according to Chapter 1 the astrological houses are essential tied to a point of mundane space beyond the axis of the World, in which anything is born, either a man or a brute animal, from this it follows that the division of the houses must be made, not for the center of the Earth, but precisely for the place of birth, so that the plane of the circles dividing the figure, cut themselves mutually in that Native in the established center of the houses.

And the reason is because the figure of the nativity is erected, so that the concourse of the virtue of the stars may be known at that point of the mundane space in which the infant is born who receives the concourse of that virtue. But he does not receive that at the center of the Earth, but on the surface of the Earth at the point where he is born; therefore, the division of the houses must be made for that point with respect to the Native himself.

But hence it follows that if any animal should be born on the surface of the Moon (as is wrongly thought [possible] by some), the *Caelum* would have to be divided for it by circles passing not through the center of the World, or the center of the Earth, nor through the center of the Moon, but through the point on the surface of the Moon on which it would be born.

You will object that the circles dividing the figure or the *Caelum*, namely the horizon, the meridian, and the circles of position, are by common consent the greatest ones. Therefore, they pass through the center of the World, but not through the child being born.

I reply. Such circles in the Native's figure are not exactly the greatest (with the exception of the meridian), but they differ from the greatest circles, and yet the difference is absolutely insensible. For if indeed the distance of the Sun from the Earth with respect to the semi-diameter of the sphere of the fixed stars is not sensible, how much less sensible will the semi-diameter of the Earth be, since the whole Earth, even full of light like the Moon, at least from the place of Jupiter or Saturn would vanish into an invisible point?

Moreover, this answer is valid for any other similar objections, so that the division of the houses is made in the equator by equilateral triangles, which however in that case will not be equilateral, nor will the individual houses differ from each other by 30 degrees of the equator, as we have proposed in Section II, Chapter 2, nor will the rising point of the ecliptic be partilely opposed to the setting point, if indeed in all of these the difference is absolutely insensible, so that as far as the effect, it doesn't matter whether the division of the houses is made for the Native's place or for the center of the World.

But from this it also follows that the true places of the planets put in the ephemerides, which are referred to the center of the Earth, ought to be corrected by parallax and reduced to the place on the surface of the Earth in which the child is born, and especially the place of the Moon, then especially when it is close to the horizon, on account of its parallax [there] of around one degree. For the Native is affected by the rays of the planets directed or hurled towards him but not to another [place].[1]

Finally, it follows that if the Earth would have increased its bulk by divine virtue, so that its diameter would be half of the diameter of the *Caelum*, but the planets would have been drawn back in the same ratio; indeed, the mode of action of the planets and the *Caelum* would not have been varied, but they would always act upon a man born upon the surface of the Earth, by reason of their own nature—of house, site, and rulership.

But the equator would be very unequally divided by circles of position, with six houses placed above the horizon and six below existing for the place of the Native on the surface of the Earth; and consequently, the triplicities of the houses would not have been established by equilateral triangles on the equator itself, and also by a notable difference, contrary to the fundamentals of the generic virtue of the houses laid down by us; which things having been abandoned, no conformable things can be established for them.

Whence, here too the divine wisdom shines forth that not only located the Earth (the natal domicile of man) in the very center of the *Caelum*, but made it as it were an insensible point with respect to the *Caelum*, so that those fundamentals would exist.

But now, since these same circles divide the *Caelum*, the Earth, and the whole mundane space similarly, it must be defined in which of those three consists primarily and per se the material cause of the houses. And indeed it is certain that it is not the *Caelum* or its parts intercepted by the circles of position, as many suppose. For the *Caelum* and its parts revolve in the diurnal motion, but the astrological houses are immobile and fixed. For however the *Caelum* moves around, the 10th house at any place on Earth begins from the fixed meridian of that place; the 1st house from the ortive [place of the] horizon [which is] also fixed; and so

---

[1]Here Morin makes a valid argument for employing the topocentric position of a planet, i.e. its position as affected by parallax, and particularly the topocentric position of the Moon, but so far as I am aware, he never did so, and nearly all astrologers before and since have ignored the correction for parallax.

with the rest [of the houses]; therefore, the *Caelum* is not the prime and material cause per se of the houses.

But similarly, that the cause is not the terrestrial globe is shown thus: for if at the impending time of birth, with God willing, a saved pregnant woman would have been annihilated, against whom some Demon would have acted upon the obstetrics, or if that Demon would have transported the pregnant woman into the uppermost regions of the air, and there he would have received the child being born, he would equally have been subject to the celestial influences with the virtue of the houses, just as would the rest who are being born on the Earth; for by these hypotheses, the mode of acting of the celestial bodies would not have been changed, but they would have flowed into the Native in accordance with the nature of the site for it.

But in these cases, the terrestrial globe cannot be the material cause of the houses. Add that the division of the houses should be made for the body of the Native primarily and per se, but not for the Earth.

And so it remains that the material cause of the houses consists of the mundane space intercepted by the two hemicycles of position, continued from the place of the Native to the uppermost surface, which space is indeed fixed and immobile even as the meridian and the rest of the circles of position dividing it are to the horizon; and the equator itself, viewed abstractly, which also preserves an immobile site in that very space and with respect to all the dividing circles.

Chapter 3. *How Many Astrological Houses there Are;*
and How Each of Them should be Defined.

Already, from what was said above, it can be clearly deduced that a duplication is given in the nature of an astrological house—namely, a primary and a secondary one.

Therefore, in general the primary one is the part of mundane space intercepted by the two hemicycles of position, either of which from the horizon or the meridian, or one from the horizon and the other from the meridian, which is distant 30 degrees on the equator. Whence, since the globe itself is divided into twelve kinds of houses—that is, the Houses of Life, Riches, Brothers, etc.—there will be in kind the primary House of Life the part of the mundane space existing between the hemicycle of the ortive horizon and another hemicycle of position beneath the Earth, distant from the horizon by 30 degrees of the equator, and so with the rest of the houses.

Therefore, the part of the mundane space is said to be the material of that house, and the rest are the differences of that essential house, including the essential relations—the location indeed with respect to the horizon and the meridian, then the Native existing in that location, but its distance to the equator, and so it excludes the location and its distance with respect to the vertical.

Moreover, that which is defined is properly called a *house*, it is necessary, as everyone acknowledges, who, in order that they may know, in what house of the figure a planet or a sign exists, to what part of the mundane space it will come by its own motion, or among which of the above said circles of position it is found, they explore by calculation or by instrument, and each planet or each part of the *Caelum* they allow to run through all the houses during their own revolution.

Moreover, a house is said to be *primary* both because from what was already said, that the astrological house of a planet is only recognized from the previously recognized space that it occupies, and then because of its virtue as the House of Life, of Wealth, and of the rest. For its space is primarily determinative by reason of its site with respect to the Native, and effectively through the space by the *Caelum* and the other celestial bodies.

For they are in different sites, so that in the case of [a particular] location, various modifications by means of which the universal virtue of the celestial bodies are modified to doing this rather than that, it is determined and reduced to a particular action, as is evidently proved in the case of the Sun, which, remaining the same in itself and with respect to the points of the equinox, only by the diversity of the site in different spheres, at the same time produces Spring, Summer, Autumn, and Winter; and again from the same Sun, which is always permitted to have the force of burning by means of a concave mirror, nor yet does it burn from every location with respect to itself, but the [image of the] Sun should be borne either to its concave axis or the concave axis should be brought to such a site; then [it is proved] by the optical tube,[1] in which unless in a certain distance of the glasses we cannot discern objects, and from numerous other distances, that neither from any distance, nor from any site at the same distance they perform the same thing, or they affect it in the same mode.[2]

Moreover, it is proved by a valid reason that the virtue of a house is primarily and per se in its space. For if the 27th degree of Aries is the significator of life since it is on the rising cusp, that cusp will therefore be much more [important] and consequently primarily and per se the significator of life, very like that on account of every single one, and that more.[3] Moreover, the sort of life is signified by the sort of the sign of the zodiac and the sort of planet that will occupy the primary house of life or will rule it.

You will object that there is no space given in the World that is not empty, because that is not admitted by Nature[4]; [and] not full, since fullness excludes space, therefore the primary houses are mere figments of the imagination.

---

[1] That is, by a *telescope*.

[2] He appears to be making an analogy between the different spaces of the *Caelum* that affect the native in different ways, and the different spacing of the *lenses* in a telescope that affect its focus on different objects.

[3] I am uncertain what he means by these last two clauses. They seem to mean that the actual ASC degree has a signification like the whole ASC but more so.

[4] Morin has in mind the saying, "Nature abhors a vacuum."

I reply. It is false that fullness excludes space, since space does not differ formally from that in which the body is, but the whole World fills up the space that it occupies [and] does not exclude its own location in which it is, and therefore not the space itself, which in vain would be said to be full, if it wasn't. Therefore, a space is given; and in the space of the World a diversity of site, and in that diversity of site a diversity of virtue, as was set forth above.

Moreover, the secondary astrological house is generally that part of the *Primum Mobile*, the beginning of which is intercepted by the circles of position of any primary house. But for example, the secondary House of Life is the part of the *Primum Mobile* intercepted at the moment of the nativity by the circles of position of the primary House of Life. This definition therefore says that there are three essentials for a secondary house: that is, it is a part of the *Primum Mobile*, [the location of] its site, and the instant of time in which it receives that site.

Moreover, as far as it says [that it is] a part of the *Primum Mobile*, it expresses its material being, and it separates that both from the lower bodies and from the mundane space. And because no part of the *Primum Caelum* is determined, it always clings to the horizon or to another circle of position on account of the continuous motion of the *Caelum* itself; therefore, each house of the secondary kind abstracts from each part of the *Primum Caelum* the things determined; otherwise, the first of these houses, which is said to be [the House] of Life, would always be the same part of the *Primum Caelum* at the moment of each nativity on the same horizon, which is absurd, since from that it would follow that neither the supreme *Caelum* nor the Earthly one is moved, therefore for different instants of revolution, by which the division of the supreme *Caelum* is made into these houses, the different parts of which are found to be intercepted by the hemicycles of the primary House of Life.

But so far, the definition says that the site of that celestial part, with respect to the horizon or to the Native himself and the time of the site, [together] indicate the formal essence of that secondary house. For not any part of the *Primum Caelum* has from itself what is this or that kind of house, as for example [the House] of Life, [the House] of Riches, etc. Since any part of the *Caelum* itself is, at the same instant of time, some kind of house in different horizons, which therefore with respect to any one horizon, that part is this or that kind of house, and [it is still] another kind of house with respect to another horizon, it formally has from the primary house of the same name, of which that part is intercepted by the circles of position in each horizon; for first and per se the virtue of the house is in the primary houses, and through them in the secondary houses, as was said above.

Besides, any particular part of the *Caelum* does not constitute a particular kind of house, that is [the House] of Life or [the House] of Riches through its own perpetual existence, or at any instant of time within the circles of position of the primary house of the same name, since it does not always exist within those, and not at any instant is a natural house made (for here we reject the fictitious divisions of the *Caelum*), but through its existence within those same circles only at that instant in which there is the beginning of any natural thing, for which the *Caelum* is divided by Nature herself into the primary houses.

For an astrologer does not divide, but he looks into the division made by Nature and considers it. Therefore, since it is non-existent at that instant, it is not at all separable from that part of the *Caelum*; (because it can never be said that that part did not exist at that instant between those circles) and so it is [plain] that that non-existence is essential to the secondary house itself, and this also, beyond its own site of the nativity, always remains the same kind of house for the Native as it was at the moment of his nativity—inherently invariable, or by reason of its own site with respect to Aries or to the equinox, and from which the entire constitution of the *Caelum* at that same moment, as the Native belongs to, so also in being preserved, in acting, suffering, and being buried, just as we have said elsewhere.

And this is the reason why all astrologers say that the Sun, for example, transits through the Native's ASC or his first house not as often as it exists by its diurnal motion on that horizon, or as often as it runs through the fixed space of the World intercepted by the circles of the primary House of Life, but only as often as by its own motion it traverses that part of the *Primum Mobile*, which at the moment of the nativity occupied the primary ASC or the primary House of Life.

Which certainly seems to be true from the fact that it is established by experience that the planets alter the things signified, for example, by the 1st house, not in individual days, even if those same [planets] in their diurnal motion run through the mundane space of the primary 1st house, but only at the time in which by their own motion they come to the part of the *Primum Mobile*, which at the hour of the nativity was found in that space.

Therefore, the three things stated above as comprising the secondary house having been suitably explained, it will be very easy to obviate any objection to the contrary. If in fact, with Pico Mirandola and Alexander De Angelis saying that a determined site of the highest *Caelum* occurs from the parts and is drawn down by the diurnal motion, and consequently that site is an essential [part] of no house; it must be replied that a part of the *Caelum* must be considered either [solely] in itself or as a part of the *Caelum*; which agreed, the site is merely accidental to it or as far as a house; which [further] agreed, the site is essential to it, as being the means by which the house exists at that instant, which is the beginning of the thing for which the *Caelum* is divided.

But to the one objecting, [we say that] no planet is at the same time in the same house of the figure for the whole Earth, but every planet is at the same time in the same part of the *Caelum* for the whole Earth. Therefore, each part of the *Caelum* is not a house of the figure. This must be rejected, as committing a sophistry from something said according to what is in the premises, to something said simply in the conclusion; for the premises are not about a house of the figure, simply from the part of the *Caelum*, but about the same house and the same part of the *Caelum*. That which, therefore, is deduced from the premises is a particular conclusion; therefore, the same part of the *Caelum* is not at the same time the same house of a figure for the whole Earth, which agrees with the truth.

Furthermore, both the primary as well as the secondary house of a figure for this reason is rightly said [to exist] in astrology, because an astrologer would judge about a primary [house] from the non-existent sign or planet or its rulership and about a secondary [house] from its site at the horizon, either posited in it or in that space. And consequently, since the whole *Caelum* and the whole space of the *Caelum* are divided into twelve houses for the sake of an individual man, it is hence evidently plain that the whole World was made for the sake of an individual man.

Chapter 4. *In which the Differences and the Harmony of Each Astrological House, Namely the Primary and the Secondary Houses is More Fully Explained.*

Both differ greatly among themselves, hence it is plain that an astrological house is not primarily any [particular] part of the *Caelum*, because in the first place whatever part of the *Caelum* is contracted to being an astrological house, it is conceded to being moved from one house to another, and therefore astrologers consider in revolutions how a part of the *Caelum* occupies a house, which at the moment of a nativity was the first or the tenth house; it is therefore something previous by way of a house in whatever part of the *Caelum*; but if it is previous by way of the house, it will therefore be the house, and consequently the astrological house is given prior to any part of the *Caelum*.

For this reason, it will not be proper to say that it is said to be moved from one house to another, because by its motion and site it is immediately this or that house, because since no part of the *Caelum* is inherently this or that house, it ought to be the kind of a house primarily from where it is. And therefore, each part of the *Caelum* is made to be one or another secondary house only by motion.

Besides, the astrological houses can also be in the entirely annihilated celestial World, so that there only remain the ethereal and elemental, for with this posited, the planets nevertheless are moved from one house to another by their own motions, and at the time of the solstices, the Equator, its poles and consequently the meridian can be determined exactly; wherefore, the natural division is also found without the *Primum Mobile*.

And if the World would have been founded in that state, the influences of the planets on man would have appeared according to the reasons of the houses, which they traverse by their own motion, since (as experience establishes) the houses determine not only parts of the *Caelum*, but also the planets to their own significations. Therefore, a house is *primarily* not any particular part of the *Caelum*; besides, for any place on Earth the circles of positions of the houses are fixed; therefore the houses of that place, of which these circles are the limits, are also fixed; therefore, the houses are not primarily parts of the *Primum Caelum*, because those are continually moving.

Besides, the same planet is at the same time in the same part of the *Caelum* for the whole Earth, especially [when it is] lacking parallax, but not in the same astrological house; therefore, an astrological house is not a part of the *Caelum*, at least not *primarily*, but only from its own site at the beginning of the origin of each thing; therefore it primarily and per se belongs to the site, which is not in any way distinguished from the *primary* house mentioned above, since it is its own formal definition.

Finally, when it is asked about any planet, in which house it is, one does not investigate under which part of the *Caelum* it is located, but in which site with respect to the Native, or between the hemicycles of which house; therefore, that which is intercepted primarily and immutably by these is *primarily* a house. Add that

111

the transits of the planets through the *primary houses* is by their common or diurnal motion, but through the *secondary houses* by their own motion; therefore, these two differ greatly. Moreover, that a house is *secondary* says that the relation of its essence to the *primary* house is as the relation of its actual efficiency to the Native.

Besides, these are the harmonies of the astrological houses. *First*, every astrological house has the same ascension everywhere on Earth, namely 30 degrees of the equator, and the same ascension in time—that is, 30 degrees of the equator ascend in just as much time in the most oblique sphere as in the right sphere. *Second*, there are different obliquities of the equator in spheres different in kind, and it divides the *Caelum* and the globe of Earth with a different inequality; and from that it results that the same house of the same kind claims for itself the greater part of the Earth or the *Caelum*, in a sphere of one kind, as it does in a sphere of another kind.

Moreover, it is the sphere that is the same in kind that has the same altitude of the same pole above the horizon; from which it follows that all those under the equator, or living under the same parallel, have the same kind of sphere. But the same sphere in number is the one that is determined through the altitude of the same pole and the same longitude on Earth, for that way it is individual.

Besides, this is worthy of note: that if the houses are quite equal in the more oblique sphere, certainly widest around the meridian and narrowest around the horizon; that is found to be well compensated by Nature. If in fact the narrower houses are nearer the zodiac, and from that they are more effective than the wider ones; whose vastness is not made notable by the presence of the planets, but only their extent around the sections of the horizon and the meridian.

Chapter 5. *Containing two Necessary Problems Relating to the Figure of the* Caelum *that has Been Erected.*

It seemed [useful] to us to add the two following Problems here—that is, because their use in astrology can not infrequently be more necessary.

Problem I.

To Find by what Perpendicular Arc any Planet is Distant from any Circle of Position of the Houses.[1]

This Problem is of great moment in astrology, so that it may be known whether a planet located on the center [itself] or only by virtue of an orb on the cusp of any house is inside or outside of that house; because the planets are significators by reason of the houses in which they are located. Therefore, because in my nativity Mercury is near the cusp of the 12th, so I am looking for its true distance from that cusp.

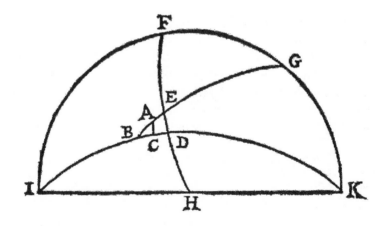

---

[1]The purpose of this Problem is to find the *mundane* position of a planet in the nativity. We are accustomed to consider only the *zodiacal* position of a planet with regard to the house cusp. But planets have latitude, and if a planet is close to a cusp in longitude, its latitude may cause its mundane position to be on one side of the cuspal line or on the other side. Here. Morin gives a geometrical procedure for discovering how far the planet is from a particular cusp.

Let the meridian be IFG, the horizon IHK, the circle of position of the 12th house IDK, the equator FH, its pole G, cutting the circle of position at D. Mercury A, with southern declination 13°57', from which to the circle IDK let the perpendicular arc AC be dropped down, the true distance of Mercury from that cusp, which is sought.

First, the oblique ascension of the 12th cusp on the point of the equator is given as 344°42' [found] namely by adding 60° to the RAMC; then E, the right ascension of Mercury is 330°43'; therefore [the arc] ED is given as 13°59'.[1]

Second, from the given FI and FD with the right angle F, FDI will be given, the complement of the altitude of the pole above IDK.

Third, in the triangle DEB, with a right angle at E, from the said ED and EDB, are given EBD as 42°35' and EB 15°43', from which EB having taken away AE 13°57', there remains AB 1°46.

Fourth, in the triangle BAC, with a right angle at C, from the given AB and ABC, is given the desired arc AC 1°12'.[2] It is, therefore, [the distance of] Mercury from the center[3] beyond the 12th house, but more in virtue in the 12th house than in the 11th house, because the strength of each house mostly flourishes in the beginning of that house, and it fades out at the end. And this I have certainly always experienced in the case of learned men and Mercu-

---

[1]Morin's horoscope has RAMC 284°27', so the OA of the 12th cusp should be 344°27', and the RA and Declination of Mercury precisely calculated from the Longitude and Latitude given in his chart are 330°50' and - 14°10'. Hence, the arc ED should be 13°37'. The divergent numbers that he gives may perhaps refer to an earlier version of his nativity.

[2]A more precise calculation, using the formulae given by Alan Leo, *Casting the Horoscope* (London: L. N. Fowler, 1970. 11th ed.), pp. 181-182, yields a Circle of Position for Mercury of 58°35', which puts the mundane position of Mercury at 1°25 from the 12th house cusp. This is not too different from the figure of 1°12' that Morin derived by his procedure. Mercury was thus still in the 11th house, but close to the 12th house cusp.

[3]That is, the *cusp.*

rial types, whom on account of envy I had rather as secret and harmful enemies, with a few exceptions among magistrates and nobles devoid of envy and endowed with by no means ordinary virtue. Moreover the arc AC for Venus is 0°12' for Venus in my same nativity.[1]

Problem II.

Problem II. *Having Been given the Longitude and Latitude of a Planet Posited in the Twelfth House, Along with its Arc of Direction to the Degree of the Ecliptic Ascending, to Find that Degree or its Oblique Ascension.*[2]

This Problem explains how to rectify the hour of the nativity by means of a direction rotating the ASC to a planet in the 12th for any kind of accident, such as death, a wound, imprisonment, exile, etc.; if that cannot be done [bodily, then] by angles to the following boundaries.

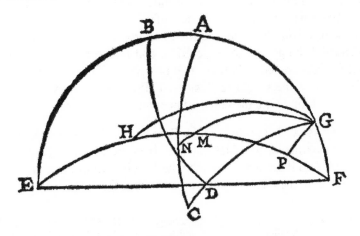

---

[1]A calculation of the mundane position of Venus yields a Circle of Position of 60°02N, or 0°02' from the cusp, so that Venus was very close to the 12th house cusp. Morin derived 0°12 as the cuspal distance using his procedure.

[2]This Problem explains a procedure for calculating converse primary directions of the planets in the 12th house to the ASC. And he says a similar procedure can be used to direct planets in the 9th house conversely to the MC. He says that these directions are particularly useful for rectifying the birth time.

Therefore, let the horizon be EDF, the meridian EGF, the equator AC, its pole G, the ecliptic BD, Saturn at H, its Circle of Position EHF, the point of the ecliptic that is sought D, or its oblique ascension, and M its place on the Circle of Position. Let it be supposed that circles of declination HG, MG, and DG are drawn through H, M, and D to the equator, and NC will be the arc of direction or the converted time of the accident in degrees of the equator; and from G let a perpendicular be dropped down to EHF as the arc GP, and this will be the altitude of the pole above the Circle of Position EHF.

Now, from the given longitude and latitude of Saturn, let its right ascension be given,[1] and therefore let its distance from the meridian be whatever, and let this be subtracted from its right ascension, and there will remain the RAMC, to which by adding 90 degrees is made the oblique ascension of the ASC degree D, to be found and preserved. Therefore, because the declination of Saturn is given, or the arc HG, and the altitude of the Pole GF, with the angle HGF, which is the complement of the semicircle of the distance of Saturn from the supposed MC; therefore, in the triangle HGF, there will be given the angle GFH; and therefore in the triangle GFP, right angled at P, there will be given GP the altitude of the Pole above the Circle of Position EHF, which however will be quickly found with the tables of positions.

And so, at that altitude of the Pole let the oblique ascension of Saturn be taken, to which let the given arc of direction NC be added. And if the sum is equal to the oblique ascension of the ASC D, taken in the circle of position of Saturn, the supposed distance

---

[1]Morin's coordinates for Saturn in his nativity are 12 ♓ 19 2S01, which yield RA 344°29' and Declination - 8°49'. And for Morin's latitude 45N25, the AD - 9°03', the SDA of Saturn 80°57'. And the natal RAMC was 284°42'. From these figures the calculation could be made as follows. The Meridian Distance was 344°29'- 284°42' = 59°47'. The RAMC when it is rising in mundo is 263°32'. Therefore the Arc of Direction is 21°10'. This corresponds to a date in the summer of 1604, and Morin noted some dangers that occurred the next year in 1605, for which see his discussion of his Solar Return for 1605 and the subsequent Lunar Return for July 1605 in AG Book 23, pp. 39-41 and 76.

of Saturn from the meridian will be true; if it is less, the distance was justly supposed to be less; finally, if it was greater, the distance was justly supposed to be greater, and the greater supposition will have to be repeated, or of the minor difference of Saturn from the meridian, until the sum is equal to the oblique ascension of the rising point D, taken in the circle of position of Saturn. Moreover, with this equality given, now let the oblique ascension of that point or of the ASC degree D be taken at the latitude of that place of the figure, and let 90 degrees be taken away from it, and there will remain the true RAMC, which Saturn will give for the true distance from the meridian lastly supposed. For in the case of this Problem, there is no direct path. Similarly the MC will be directed conversely to a planet in the 9th house for rectification.

Chapter 6. *Some Divisions of the Houses or the Celestial Figure.*

The houses of the celestial figure are divided primarily into oriental and occidental houses. There are six oriental houses, namely the 3rd, 2nd, 1st, 12th, 11th, and 10th, which also is called the oriental half of the figure, because the planets in this half rise with respect to the Native. But the remaining six houses are occidental, [namely] the 9th, 8th, 7th, 6th, 5th, and 4th, which is also called the occidental half of the figure because through it the planets descend from the vertex.

Secondly, they are divided into four quadrants. And the first quadrant contains the houses 12, 11, and 10; and it is called oriental, vernal, masculine, bloody, and belonging to childhood. The second quadrant has houses 9, 8, and 7; and it is called meridional, summer, feminine, choleric, and youthful. The third quadrant contains houses 6, 5, and 4; and it is called occidental, autumnal, masculine, melancholic, and virile. Finally, the fourth quadrant claims houses 3, 2, and 1; and it is called wintry, feminine, phlegmatic, and elderly.

Which [you] understand [is] according to the old astrologers;

but it seems absurd that the second quadrant is feminine; and the 1st house, from which is the beginning of mundane life, is located in the elderly quadrant and not rather in the childhood quadrant.

Thirdly, they are divided into angular, succedent, and cadent houses. The angular houses are 1, 10, 7, and 4. The succedent houses are 2, 5, 8, and 11. But the cadent houses are 3, 6, 9, and 12. Concerning which, see Book 16, Chapter 4. Nevertheless, it must be noted here that the cardinal, succedent, and cadent houses are disposed in a figure according to the second motion of the planets, or from the setting to the rising; and the 2nd house is succedent, and the 3rd is cadent with respect to the 1st.[1]

But by the prime motion from the rising to the setting, a planet going out of the 1st house enters a house that is cadent with respect to the 10th,[2] and then into a succedent. And yet, it should not therefore be said to be cadent or succedent, for these appellations do not properly suit the planets but rather the houses; and it must not be thought as some do that a planet is very weak in a cadent house, and that its strength is continually increased when by the diurnal motion it proceeds to the following angle in which it is strongest. For Saturn in the 12th is stronger for the things signified for the subjects of the 12th, which are illnesses, imprisonments, enemies, etc., than in the 10th for the subjects of the 10th, especially if its celestial state is badly afflicted; and so with the rest [of the planets].

End of Book 17.

---

[1]This is not the original definition! Properly speaking, the 3rd house is cadent with respect to the 4th house because *cadent* means 'falling away from [an angle]', and plainly the 3rd house is falling away from the 4th house, not the 1st house. Morin was perhaps misled by the phrase often used by the classical astrologers 'cadent from the ASC', which was applied to all of the cadent houses 3, 6, 9, and 12; but the mention of 'the ascendant' in the phrase was merely a reminder that the term *cadent* referred to a chart in which the ASC was the 1st house.

[2]Not so! As explained in the preceding note, it enters into the 12th house, which is cadent from the 1st house, not cadent from the 10th.

Index of Persons

Koch, Walther, astrologer, 87n.1

Leo, Alan, astrologer, NOT FOUND

Lesdiguières, François de Bonne, Duke of, Constable of France, 54n.1,79-80

Mirandola, Giovanni II Pico, Lord of, 8,9,20,21,109

Negusantius, astrologer, 92n.1

Offusius, Jofrancus, astrologer, xiii,40,82

Placidus de Titis, astrologer, ix,74n.1,87n.1

Plotinus, philosopher, 8,20

Porphyry, philosopher, 69,71,87n.1

Ptolemy, Claudius, astrologer, xii-ix,7,9,19,20,38,43,39n.1,71,82,86,92,99

Regiomontanus, astronomer, ix,x,6n.2,38n.2,41n.1,42,47n.1, 47n.2,48n.1,74n.1,85,86n.1,87n.1,97

Richelieu, Armand du Plessis, Cardinal, 56,57

Riske, Kris B, editor, xiii

Robbins, F. E., translator, xii

Thorndike, Lynn, historian, 6n.1,70n.3,82n.2

Valois, Jacques, treasurer, 79

Villennes, Nicolas de Bourdin, Marquess of, astrologer, 42n.3,99n.3

Virgil, poet, 60

Wallenstein, Albert of, Duke of Mecklenburg, general, x,65n.1,66n.2

Wharton, Sir George, astrologer, xiin.1

Note: the characterization given for each person is not necessarily complete, but it represents the type of work that he did to which reference is made in the Preface or in the Translation or the footnotes. Book publishers' names are not listed. They may be found in the Bibliography.

Bibliography

Alchabitius (Abû al-Saqr al-Qabîsî)
  Alcabitii ad magisterium iudiciorum astrorum.
  [Alchabitius's Book on the Art of Judgments of the Stars]
  Paris: Simon de Colines, 1521.

Angelis, Alexander de, Father (Angeli, Allesandro degli)
  In Astrologos coniectores. Libri Quinque.
  [Conjectures against the Astrologers. Five Books.]
  Lyons: H. Cardon, 1615. 4to xxviii,351,xxxi pp.
  Rome: B. Zanetti, 1615. 2nd ed. 4to

Aquinas, Thomas, Saint
  Summa Theologica.
  [Theological Summary]
  various editions

Augustine, Saint
  De civitate Dei.
  [The City of God.]
  [Latin text and English translation]
  The Loeb Classical Library
  London: Wm. Heinemann and
  Cambridge, Mass.: Harvard Univ. Press, 1960. 7 vols. repr.

Cardan, Jerome
  Claudii Ptolemaei Pelusiensis libri quatuor/
  De astrorum iudiciis cum expositione Hieronoymi Cardani.
  [Cardan's Commentary on the Quadripartite.]
  in vol. 5 of Cardan's
  Opera Omnia.
  Lyons: Huguetan & Ravaud, 1662. 10 vols.
  London: Johnson Reprint, 1967. 10 vols. reprint of 1662

Haly ('Alî ibn abi al-Rijâl)
Liber completus de iudiciis astrorum.
[The Complete Book on the Judgments of the Stars]
Venice: J. B. Sessa, 1503. often reprinted

Hermes the Philosopher (actually Albumasar)
De revolutionibus nativitatum.
[The Revolutions of Nativities]
Basel: Petriana, 1559. folio

Jerome, Saint, Translator
Biblia Sacra Juxta Vulgatam Clementinam.
[The Holy Bible According to the Clementine Vulgate]
Rome, Tournai, Paris: Desclée & Co., 1947. xli,1280,288,152
maps diagrs.

Leo, Alan
Casting the Horoscope.
London: L. N. Fowler, 1970. 11th ed. 4to xxviii,354 pp.
diagrs. tables

Mirandola, Giovanni Pico della, Count
Disputationes adversus astrologiam.
[Disputations Against Astrology]
Bologna: Benedictus Hectoris, 1496.

Morin, Jean Baptiste
Astrologicarum domorum cabala detecta
a Joanne Baptista Morino...
[The Cabala of the Astrological Houses
Discovered by Jean Baptiste Morin...]
Paris: J. Moreau, 1623. 8vo 38 pp. diagrs.

Tabulae Rudolphinae...supputatae
a Joanne Baptista Morino...
[The Rudolphine Tables...Calculated

by Jean Baptiste Morin...]
Paris: J. Lebrun, 1650. quarto 117 pp. tables

Les Remarqves Astrologiqves...
Paris: Pierre Menard, 1657. quarto 168 pp.

Remarques Astrologiques...
with an introduction and notes
by Jacques Halbronn
Paris: Retz, 1975. modern ed. 303 pp. portr. diagrs. tables

Astrologia Gallica.
The Hague: Adrian Vlacq, 1661. folio xxxvi,784 pp. portr. diagrs. tables

Books 13-15 & 19.
trans. by James Herschel Holden
Tempe, Az.: A.F.A., Inc., 2006. paper iv,300 pp. diagrs tables 22 cm.

Book 18 – The Strengths of the Planets.
trans. by Pepita Sanchis Llacer and Anthony Louis LaBruzza
Tempe, Az.: A.F.A., Inc., 2004. paper 101 pp. port. diagrs

Book 21 – Determinations.
The Morinus System of Horoscopic Interpretation.
trans. by Richard S. Baldwin
Washington: A.F.A., Inc., 1974. paper [v],109 pp.
Tempe, Az: A.F.A., Inc., 2008, repr. paper viii, 144 pp.

Book 22 – Primary Directions.
trans. by James Herschel Holden
Tempe, Az.: A.F.A., Inc., 1992. paper xv,292 pp. 21 cm.
Tempe, Az.: A.F.A., Inc., 2005. repr. paper xv,292 pp. 21 cm.

Book 23 – Revolutions.
trans. by James Herschel Holden
Tempe, Az.: A.F.A., Inc., 2003. 1st ed. paper x,142 pp. portr.
diagrs. tables 28 cm.
Tempe, Az.: A.F.A., Inc., 2004. 2nd ed. rev. paper portr.
diagrs. tables

Book 24 – Progressions and Transits.
trans. by James Herschel Holden
Tempe, Az.: A.F.A., Inc., 2005. paper xii,111 pp. diagrs.
tables 21 cm.

Book 25 – De Constitutionibus Coeli Universalibus.
[The Universal Constitutions of the Caelum]
trans. into French by Jean Hieroz as
L'Astrologie mondiale et météorologique
de Morin De Villefranche.
[The Mundane and Meteorological Astrology
of Morin of Villefranche]
Paris : Les Éditions Leymarie, 1946. paper 176 pp.

Offusius, JoFrancus
De divina astrorum facultate in
larvatam astrologiam.
[The Divine Power of the Stars Against
a Decadent Astrology]
Paris, 1570.

Ptolemy, Claudius
Tetrabiblos.
ed. & trans. by F. E. Robbins
The Loeb Classical Library
London: Wm. Heinemann and
Cambridge, Mass.: Harvard Univ. Press, 1940. xxiv,466 pp.

Regiomontanus
  Tabulae directionum profectionumque...
  In nativitatibus multum utiles.
  [Tables of Directions and Profectiuons...
  Very Useful in Nativities]
  Augsburg: Erhard Ratdolt, 1490. 4to

Thorndike, Lynn
    Latin Treatises on Comets Between 1238 and 1368 A.D.
    Chicago: The Univ. of Chicago Press, 1950).

    A History of Magic and Experimental Science.
    [cited as HMES]
    New York: Columbia University, 1923-1958. 8 vols.